TEACHING READING
IN
COMPENSATORY CLASSES

edited by
ROBERT C. CALFEE
Stanford University
and
PRISCILLA A. DRUM
University of California
at Santa Barbara

INTERNATIONAL
READING
ASSOCIATION
800 Barksdale Road
Newark, Delaware 19711

INTERNATIONAL READING ASSOCIATION

Copyright 1979 by the
International Reading Association, Inc.

Library of Congress Cataloging in Publication Data
Main entry under title:

Teaching reading in compensatory classes.

    Bibliography: p.
    1. Reading—United States—Addresses, essays,
lectures. 2. Compensatory education—United
States—Addresses, essays, lectures. I. Calfee,
Robert C. II. Drum, Priscilla A.
LB1050.T37   371.9'67   79-10110
ISBN 0-87207-725-X

CONTENTS

Foreword

The International Reading Association became involved in the publication of *Teaching Reading in Compensatory Classes* in rather unusual fashion. Many months ago Roger Farr informed his fellow members of the IRA Board of Directors that he had been serving as a consultant to a project that would yield "a mountain of data" which IRA could—and perhaps should—acquire and interpret for the benefit of its members and the profession at large.

At the time of Farr's pronouncement to the Board, the data were in possession of the U.S. Office of Education and the Educational Testing Service, because USOE had earlier given ETS a contract to carry out a four-year study of compensatory reading instruction in the United States.

The Directors of IRA responded to Farr's report with authorization for the appointment of a committee to interact with the ETS personnel who had managed the four-year study. In the course of a couple of two-day visits to ETS headquarters, the committee considered schemes for the organization of the immense volume of data, developed an outline for a publication based on those data, and began production of several first draft chapters. However, because the authors were located in various U.S. cities, without easy or frequent access to one another for editorial and philosophical collaboration, their draft chapters became markedly different in approach and in writing style. In short, they didn't fit together, and the prospect of developing a workable total manuscript by committee seemed minimal.

Realizing that the process of authoring a book "by committee" was not working in this case, Farr and IRA Research Director John Guthrie convinced the IRA Directors that the tasks of pulling the chapters together in a unified manuscript should be turned over to an editorial staff which was familiar with sophisticated concepts of both research and reading. Thereupon the Board authorized Guthrie to seek such an editorial staff, and to negotiate with it for the completion of the manuscript which had been started by the committee. Robert Calfee and Patricia Drum accepted the assignment to manage the refinement and completion of the manuscript which led to publication of the book you are now reading.

From the foregoing it is readily apparent that *Teaching Reading in Compensatory Classes* is the product of greater-than-usual cooperation among elements of the U.S. Office of Education, the Educational Testing Service, the Stanford Center for Research and Development in Teaching, and the International Reading Association. The IRA Directors are immensely grateful to the individuals and agencies whose combined efforts have created this book.

William Eller
State University of New York at Buffalo

Preface

This book examines the Educational Testing Service study of compensatory reading programs. These programs represent both federal and state support through legislation and budget allocations. Many school districts receive some type of compensatory funding in order to improve the reading performance of children from low income families—low income and low academic performance are highly correlated. Once a district has received funding for this purpose and a special program is implemented, most pupils with below average skills receive aid from the special services. The amounts received by any given districts may seem small, but when summed over all U.S. school districts, it is "big business."

The Educational Testing Service study describes reading programs resulting from these special allocations. The data from this study were reported to the U.S. Office of Education a few years ago. However, technical reports are sometimes difficult to obtain and often difficult to interpret. The major aim of this book is to make these results available to administrators, legislators, teachers, and others responsible for funding, planning, and implementing compensatory reading programs.

This book stresses the evidence collected about the teachers, the pupils, and the instructional programs involved in compensatory reading. Every effort is made to base interpretations on the original data. Authors have turned to their professional expertise to add historical comparisons, additional evidence, and evaluations of the adequacy of program characteristics. However, the book is chiefly based on data.

We have tried to make the evidence clear and the explanations readable. To be sure, the descriptions of the methods for summarizing the data and the account of the actual findings require attention and thoughtful reading. This book is intended for those who will make decisions about compensatory programs. Research evidence is only one source for making such decisions, but a careful evaluation of the evidence should provide a reasonable basis for reaching informed decisions.

We have had the responsibility for tying together the contributions of the several authors. Without the patient cooperation of everyone, the work would never have been completed. Original drafts had to be rewritten when we noted that the *compensatory versus noncompensatory* classification was suspect (Chapter 1). This discovery led to a complete reanalysis and major revisions. This effort depended on the authors' standards of quality and willingness to make an added effort in order to ensure an accurate report. We are most appreciative of their patience and hard work.

Roger Farr and William Eller foresaw the Compensatory Reading Study data as a potentially important source of information to the reading profession. It was through their efforts that the International Reading Association made the arrangements for this project with the Educational Testing Service. The Association provided the support for the project, and throughout we have had the benefit of guidance from John Guthrie, Research Director of the Association, and the IRA Advisory Group on Analysis of Reading Program Data, which included Richard L. Allington, Roger Farr, John T. Guthrie, Diane J. Sawyer, Sam Weintraub, and Gita Wilder.

We are most grateful to Jay Thorp for her talented assistance in preparing the manuscript, the figures, and the tables. The theoretical and methodological basis for the work in Chapters 8 and 9 was made possible by a grant from the Carnegie Corporation to R. Calfee.

RCC
PAD

Chapter 1

The Compensatory Reading Survey

Priscilla A. Drum
University of California at Santa Barbara
Robert C. Calfee
Stanford University

Background

The American public expects that, after six years of school instruction, a child should be able to read with fluency and understanding. Most students meet this expectation reasonably well. Other students are less successful. The actual rate of illiteracy depends on the criteria for defining it. For instance, Grant and Lind (1975) report that illiteracy dropped from twenty percent in 1870 to less than one percent in 1969, an encouraging accomplishment over a century. However, they are referring to the percentage of people 14 years or older who can read some message in some language. Other data suggest that a sizable percentage of the nation's citizens have problems reading simple, everyday materials. For instance, Golladay (1976) found that 22 percent of the 17-year-olds sampled could not respond adequately to the information printed on a traffic ticket. These criteria are certainly minimal and do not reflect the needs of tomorrow's society. More to the point, a student might be literate by this criterion, but unable to understand many of the texts used in secondary schools.

The benefits of education, as indicated by skilled reading achievement, are not equally distributed over all sectors of our society. In particular, educational attainment is strongly correlated with family socioeconomic status (Grant & Lind, 1975). The exact causal links may elude researchers, but the general sense is that poverty and low academic achievement are intertwined in a continuous link which has proven resistant to intervention.

Title I of the Elementary and Secondary Education Act of 1965 sought to break this vicious circle by the establishment of compensatory education programs for disadvantaged students:

> Congress hereby declares it to be the policy of the United States to provide financial assistance to local educational agencies serving areas with concentration of children from low-income families in order to expand and improve their educational programs by various means . . . which contribute particularly to meeting the special educational needs of educationally deprived children. (Elementary and Secondary Education Act of 1966, PL 89-10)

How effective have been the Federal efforts at compensatory education? Numerous surveys have aimed to answer this question, with generally mixed and uncertain results (Rand, 1978).

Title I funds were distributed to 14,000 local educational districts in 1976-77. The intention was to provide incremental financial assistance to low income areas, and not to supplant state and local funding. The additional dollars were to help the schools to provide special services for low-achieving children, "to contribute to the cognitive, emotional, social, or physical development of participating students" (NIE, 1977, p. xiv). The actual implementation of "special services" varied by state and by district.

State reports, required by the Elementary and Secondary Education Act, and surveys by independent agencies evaluated the effects of Title I funding. These data have not yielded an interpretable picture of the educational value of the Title I program. Some state reports inflated the size of the population served by counting students anew for each service extended. Others indicated costs by an indeterminant combination of expenses incurred, planned expenses, and future allocations. In most cases, special services were simply described as instruction in skill areas, such as reading and mathematics. Effects of Title I funding on learning in basic areas were difficult to demonstrate. The request for achievement data confronted the reluctance or inability of school districts to provide it. Usable achievement data were obtained for less than 10 percent of the sample "in the 1968 to 1971 annual surveys conducted by the Office of Education" (NIE, 1977, p. 5).

The data are fragmented and though one can find exemplary evaluations, the nationwide effects of this important educational bill remain indeterminate. The idea of providing supplemental funds to alter and augment instruction for the economically and educationally needy student is still a politically viable policy. The Educational Testing Service (ETS) survey, which is the basis for the reports in this volume, should have permitted an examination of some of the changes in school organization, in teaching practices, and in the reading curriculum that were planned under Title I to meet the needs of disadvantaged students. Unfortunately, as we shall see, it is not easy to isolate Title I Compensatory Reading programs from other efforts to augment reading instruction for students in need.

The ETS Study of Compensatory Reading

In July 1971, ETS undertook a nationwide survey of compensatory reading programs (Rubin, Trismen, Wilder, & Yates, 1973). Designed as the first phase of a larger investigation, the survey covered more than 500 elementary school principals and over 2,000 teachers. Questionnaires asked about the school and the neighborhood, the background and training of the teachers, and the nature of instructional programs in reading.

Schools and classrooms selected for the survey represented instances of "reading instruction provided to students because they are reading below their grade level" (Rubin et al., 1973). Low achievement carried more weight in the definition of "compensatory program" than did substandard family income.

Educational Testing Service completed the preliminary analyses for the Phase I Report in August 1973 (Rubin et al., 1973). A technical report was prepared, giving descriptive summary and statistics on school and program questionnaires, based on the responses of 537 principals and 1602 teachers. The responses of teachers in ungraded classes were not included in the analysis. The impact of the 188 "no response" schools was examined; weighted frequencies were used to estimate the likely effects of the missing data.

Technical reports are seldom well suited to the needs of practitioners, and such was the case here. A number of consultants to ETS in the design of the questionnaires were members of the International Reading Association (IRA). They thought that the survey results were important and would be of interest to many professionals. With the support of ETS, they encouraged the IRA leadership to arrange for an analysis and report closer to the needs of the field for information. Subsequently, the Association was commissioned by the National Institute of Education to prepare a descriptive and interpretive study of the results. The narrative was to elaborate on the findings, focusing on what could be learned from present practice about reading instruction for the less able student, the underachiever, and children from economically deprived communities.

The First R

A precedent for the present survey of compensatory reading instruction can be found in *The First R: The Harvard Report on Reading in Elementary Schools,* carried out by Austin and Morrison (1963). They presented results and thoughtful interpretations from questionnaire data based on a national sample of elementary school principals and district superintendents. The report described the instructional methods, techniques, and materials used in the elementary schools, the inservice training provided for teachers, and the role of administrators in improving the reading instruction in the public schools. However, *The First R* did not differentiate between reading programs designed for average as contrasted with below average groups.

Austin and Morrison found that the most prevalent approach in 1963 was to divide children into three reading ability groups, maintaining these groups intact through the school year. Continuous assessment and regrouping for specific instruction were practiced by a modest number of teachers. The instructional program was dictated by a basal reading series and the accompanying manual. Austin and Morrison felt that improvements in reading instruction were unlikely to be instigated by administrative leadership; most principals lacked the time and the training to help teachers improve. The authors believed that their survey showed a clear need for improved preservice training for elementary teachers, designed to help them plan their reading instruction to meet the needs of individual students. A followup survey suggested that there was some change along these lines during the past ten years (Morrison & Austin, 1977).

The principals did believe that "poor instruction was not as much of a contributing factor as environmental influences. Most frequently they said that lack of home interest and the meager background that many children brought to their educational tasks hindered progress in reading. They also cited teacher and pupil mobility, parental pressure, broken homes, poor attendance, and language barriers as additional difficulties which the school must overcome" (Austin & Morrison, 1963, p. 211).

We will see below that where comparisons can be made with the ETS survey, the findings are quite similar to those in *The First R*. Reading groups within a class are still based on general reading ability; the groups, once formed, are seldom changed during the school year. The principals in the ETS survey did not answer many of the questions about their compensatory reading programs. Either the principals did not know the answers, or did not consider it worth their time and effort to investigate the question. In either case, the failure to provide answers makes one wonder about the leadership role of the principals in improving compensatory reading programs.

The First R looked at more aspects of reading instruction than did the ETS survey. For instance, it covered school and class libraries, the evaluation and reporting of pupil progress, and programs for the average and gifted student. On the other hand, Austin and Morrison sent questionnaires only to the administrative officer, the district superintendent or a delegate, and a representative principal in each school district; they did not include teachers in the survey. In the ETS study, we learn less about the school's overall reading program, but we learn more about the teachers, the pupils, the school, and the community.

Plan of the Study

In this section we describe how the ETS Phase I sample was drawn, the makeup of the questionnaires, and procedures for the distribution of the teacher questionnaires.

Design of Sample Selection[1]

The population of schools consisted of the School Universe, an annual compilation of state reports received by the National Center for Educational Statistics in Washington. Schools were initially stratified according to average family income, determined chiefly by the 1960 census median family income data. A second stratification variable was minority enrollment. The two stratification variables were selected because of findings that socioeconomic status of the community and racial-ethnic membership were highly correlated with test performance (e.g., Mayeske, Wisler, Beaton, Weinfeld, Cohen, Okaha, Proshek, & Tabler, 1972). Since number of students is often the basis for allocating funds and personnel, each set of schools was further divided into approximately equal sets based on the school-size variable. Schools were then randomly selected from each final stratum, along with substitute schools to be used if a target school refused to participate, or if the school had been in the Anchor Test Study or the Follow Through Program.

Table 1-1 shows the number of schools in each socioeconomic stratum of the sample, as well as the number of schools that were closed or failed to respond. The number of Title I schools is also indicated.[2] Table 1-2 presents the breakdown of responding schools on the minority enrollment variable.

The schools in the sample came from a broad range of regions of the country, and wide variation in urbanization was represented within each geographic region. The original file of schools provided a detailed breakdown according to degree of urbanization (Table 1-3). For most of our analyses, we have used the simpler designations of urban, suburban, and rural (categories of approximately equal size). As you can see, the distribution of teachers over geographic regions was fairly equal, except for the unexpectedly small representation of urban schools in the Northeast (Table 1-4).

Educational Testing Service sent letters to each state's chief school officer, requesting state participation and to the district superintendents of the 731 schools in the original sample. After obtaining consent from the superintendents, the principals were sent a description of the study and

---

[1] See Appendix A of the Phase I Report (Rubin, et al., 1973) for further detail.
[2] The Office of Education contract specified that 60 percent of the schools sampled should have Title I funding. Participation in Title I provides federal funding for compensatory programs, but many of these were not reading programs. A compensatory reading program was defined as "any reading instruction provided to students because they are reading below grade level," and 80 percent of the principals said they had such a program. However, many schools had other sources of funding for compensatory reading besides Title I, and some had no external funding at all. Only a third of the schools funded all compensatory reading from Title I sources. There was no direct link between Title I funding and programs, and so we have disregarded this variable in our analysis.

Table 1-1
Distribution of Schools in Sample by
Income, Response, and Title I Designation

Average Community Income in $1000	Total Sampled	Number Closed	Number No Response	Number Responding	Number of Title I
2 – 3.9	48	0	16	32	32
4 – 4.9	120	11	34	75	39
5 – 5.9	146	3	40	103	77
6 – 6.9	184	13	28	148	92
6 – 10+	222	0	50	172	76
Unclassified	11	0	6	5	0
Total	731	27	174	535	316

Table 1-2
Distribution of Schools by Percentage
of Minority Enrollment (Total N = 535)

Percent Minority Enrollment	Schools N	%
Under 5	252	47
5 – 9	75	14
10 – 19	70	13
20 – 39	64	12
40 – 59	21	4
60 – 79	21	4
Over 80	32	6

Drum and Calfee

Table 1-3
Table 1-3
Distribution of Teachers by Degree of Urbanization
(N = 1854)

Degree of Urbanization	Percent of Teachers	
Urban	**23**	
City 500K+		08
City 200-500K		06
City 50-200K		05
City Under 50K		04
Suburban	**38**	
Suburb/Large City Over 200K		10
Suburb/City 50-200K		28
Rural	**29**	
Rural/Large City Over 200K		16
Rural/City 50-200K		02
Rural		11
No Information	**10**	

conditions for participation. The teachers were guaranteed anonymity, and were told they would receive an honorarium for completing and returning the questionnaires. These procedures were successful in gaining the cooperation of 75 percent of the principals (Table 1-1).

The Questionnaires

With the help and advice of several experts in the field of reading, ETS developed three questionnaires in the Fall of 1971 (see Appendix A). First, the experts created a list of variables affecting reading achievement. These variables fell into four general categories: the characteristics of the school and the community; the characteristics of the pupils; the training, experience, and attitude of the teachers; and the organization, activities, goals, and materials for reading instruction. The principals responded to the first two categories and the teachers to all but the first one.

Table 1-4
Percent Distribution of Teachers by Geographic Region
and Urban, Suburban, and Rural Locations (N = 1854)

| Locations | Geographic Regions | | | | Total Location |
	Northeast	North Central	South	West	
Urban	03	07	06	07	23
Suburban	09	11	09	09	38
Rural	04	11	10	04	29
No Information	04	03	02	01	10
Total Region	20	32	28	21	

The Principal Questionnaire

The first eighteen items on the questionnaire asked the principal for information about the school and community. First, the principal was asked about characteristics of the school, number of students, grades, classrooms, and ratings of the adequacy of the physical facilities, the instructional and noninstructional staffs, and the instructional materials. Ninety percent of the principals responded to these questions. Next was a set of items on family income, job level, educational attainment, minority membership, home language, mobility, and amount of busing. The last set of items in this section asked the principal to identify the percent and number of students reading below grade level. Approximately half of the principals answered these last two sets of questions.

Question 19, which asked the principal whether he had a compensatory reading program, was critical in the distribution of questionnaires to teachers, as we shall see below. Eighty-nine percent of the principals in the sample indicated that there was a compensatory reading program in the school.

Items 20 through 32 asked the principal about the number of programs, when each began, the number of students, the sources of funding, costs of programs, and annual expenditures per student for each individual program. The response rate to these questions, especially those items requesting dollar estimates of expenditures and costs, was quite poor (Table 1-5). In general, less than half the principals answered any given question, and the response rate for costs was less than one out of four.

Table 1-5

Percent of Principals' Answers to Questions
on Expenditures, Costs, and Funding
(Number of Principals with Compensatory
Reading Programs = 475)

Expenditures	% Answers	Costs[a]	% Answers	Level of Funding[a]	% Answers
Question 23: School	38	Question 27: Total	15	Question 32: Federal	69
Question 24: District	51	Personnel	22	State	47
Question 26: Compensatory	24	Other	14	Local	53

[a]Data for Program 1 only. Principals with a second program (N=257) answered at about the same rate. Less than one fourth of the principals reported more than two programs.

Items 33 to 40 asked the principal how students were selected for participation in the programs, whether community and teacher resistance was encountered, and how many and what kinds of personnel had received inservice training in the last year. The response rate to these questions was generally 50 percent or higher.

Teacher Questionnaire

This form asked the teacher to provide information about professional training, years of experience, as well as attitudes toward the specific school, toward compensatory programs, and toward the academic capabilities of disadvantaged children. All teachers responsible for compensatory reading for grades two, four, and six completed this questionnaire. The 16 questions were straightforward, and most teachers answered all of them.

Class and Program Questionnaires

The class and program questionnaire was the most extensive component of the survey. The class section asked the teacher for information on class size, previous pupil training, racial-ethnic background of the pupils, family occupations, attendance records, pupil problems, pupil capability and expected educational attainment. The program section examined goals for reading activities, materials, extra instructional help, grouping procedures, and the teacher's opinion about the success of the program.

Two forms of the class and program questionnaires were prepared, one for compensatory reading programs and one for regular reading programs. Except for the word "compensatory" and two questions specific to compensatory reading, the two forms were designed to be identical. There were some other slight differences, which will be discussed below. However, the problem of comparing the forms is secondary to the greater problem of the distribution of the questionnaires, which we discuss next.

Distribution of Questionnaires

As far as we can tell, the original intent of the study was to obtain questionnaire responses from both compensatory and regular reading classes in the sample. A compensatory reading class was defined as any group of students receiving some type of "special" reading instruction due to their below-average reading performance. Regular reading classes would include groups of students reading at grade level or above, or below-average classes not receiving special reading instruction.

The principal had the task of designating compensatory reading classes through the process of distributing the questionnaires. This was not a simple task, as can be seen from the instructions to the principal:

19. Does your school conduct at least one compensatory reading program as defined?
    1 Yes If so, please go on to question 21 and complete the remainder of this questionnaire. At the same time, please, distribute questionnaires in the manner prescribed below.
    2 No If not, DO NOT COMPLETE THIS QUESTIONNAIRE. HOWEVER, PLEASE ARRANGE FOR TEACHER QUESTIONNAIRES TO BE COMPLETED BY *ONE* TEACHER OF *EACH* OF GRADES 2, 4, and 6 (3 teachers in all) HAVING THE CLASS WITH THE LOWEST AVERAGE READING ACHIEVEMENT. These teachers should receive Teacher Characteristics Questionnaires (tan) and Class and Program Characteristics Questionnaires (yellow).

DISTRIBUTION OF QUESTIONNAIRES IN SCHOOLS HAVING ONE OR MORE COMPENSATORY READING PROGRAMS AS DEFINED:
1. Questionnaires should be distributed to all teachers of compensatory reading in grades 2, 4, and 6, AND to the ONE teacher in EACH of grades 2, 4, and 6 having the class with the lowest average reading achievement. All teachers to whom questionnaires are to be distributed should receive at least two questionnaires, one Teacher Characteristics Questionnaire (tan) and one Class and Program Characteristics Questionnaire (blue and yellow).
2. Teachers of compensatory reading should be given *blue* Class and Program Characteristics Questionnaires; the teachers of grades 2, 4, and 6 whose classes have the lowest average reading achievement should be given *yellow* Class and Program Characteristics Questionnaires.
3. If teachers are involved in more than one Compensatory Reading Program (see definitions above), they should be given separate *blue* Class and Program Characteristics Questionnaires for each program in which they teach 2nd, 4th, and 6th graders.
4. If compensatory reading teachers teach pupils at more than one grade level, they should be given separate *blue* Class and Program Characteristics Questionnaires for each grade level (2, 4, and/or 6) at which they teach.

The principal first had to decide whether his school had any compensatory programs. If the school had one or more programs, he was to distribute *compensatory* questionnaires to the teachers of *all* second grade, fourth grade, sixth grade, and ungraded groups who taught such classes. He was also to distribute *regular* questionnaires to the teachers with the "lowest average reading performance" in grades two, four, and six in the school. If the principal decided that there were no compensatory reading programs in the school, then he was to distribute regular questionnaires to the teachers of the class with the "lowest average reading performance" in the second, fourth, and sixth grades.

That principals were obviously confused by these instructions shows in the way they distributed the questionnaires. Many teachers filled out both compensatory and regular questionnaires. Teachers of the lowest classes in some schools appear to have filled out only the regular forms. Some teachers were responsible for more than one class. Multiple forms for a particular teacher sometimes refer to the same class, while other times the forms are for different classes. In short, instructions to the principal concerning distribution of the questionnaires were confusing and ambiguous, and the resulting problems raise questions about the meaning of a "regular" class.

In the section that follows, we discuss how we resolved the ambiguities and discrepancies in the data base. Our general approach was to classify a class as "compensatory" if there was any positive indication that this designation was appropriate. Taking this approach meant that a few regular classes may have been improperly categorized as compensatory. Given the way that "regular" classes were designated—"lowest average reading performance"—we do not think that the misclassification is noticeably inappropriate.

By and large, we limit comparisons in this volume to the similarities and differences within compensatory reading programs. Data were available for a small number of regular schools and classes. However, because of the ambiguities in the distribution of the teacher questionnaires, we do not believe that these data are representative of regular schools and classes in general. Therefore, we will *not* draw comparisons between compensatory and regular programs, in most instances. We can describe what is being done for below-average readers; the data do not allow us to discuss how compensatory programs differ from programs aimed for students reading at grade level or above.

Reanalysis of the Study

The Phase I Report by ETS (Rubin, et al., 1973) provided basic descriptions of the survey results. The reports in the present book are based on a more detailed reanalysis. Before the reanalysis was carried out, we devised procedures for settling some of the problems mentioned above. These procedures are described in this section.

One or Two Groups of Teachers?

The first question to be resolved in the reanalysis was how to decide on classification of compensatory and regular classes. The ambiguities of the Phase I distribution procedure required a closer examination of the data.

We first determined the number of teachers completing each type of questionnaire: 1100 compensatory-only records, 598 regular-only records, 334 compensatory and regular records, 55 records with neither form completed—a total of 2087 teacher-class records.

The 1100 teachers who filled out only compensatory records posed no problem in reanalysis. These records make up the core of the survey.

The 55 teachers who filled out only a teacher-characteristics form, but neither of the program forms, appeared to be in team-teaching situations, where "one Class and Program Characteristics Questionnaire per group of students" was distributed as called for by question 19 of the principal's questionnaire. These 55 records were disregarded in the reanalysis, because there was no way to link the teacher to a class. We assumed that the teacher with primary responsibility for teaching also filled out the program questionnaire.

Next we dealt with the 334 teachers who filled out both compensatory and regular questionnaires. It often appeared that the same class was being described by the two questionnaires when we compared class size, the number of boys and girls, and the ages of the oldest and the youngest. The following sample from a teacher is typical:

Form	Class Size	Number of Boys	Number of Girls	Age Range
Compensatory	31	18	13	13.2 - 9.4
Regular	31	18	13	13.2 - 9.4

We chose to assume that, when the responses to these questions were identical, the teacher was describing the same class. By this criterion, the same class was being described on two questionnaires in 298 of the 334 classes. We used the compensatory questionnaire responses for these instances. In the remaining 36 cases, exact identification was often difficult and sometimes impossible. Some of these teachers may have actually taught two classes, but we decided to retain only the compensatory responses in the reanalysis.

The 598 teachers who filled out regular forms only posed some unique problems of their own. In 106 instances the principal said that he did *not* have a compensatory program in the school. It was therefore reasonable to classify these as regular classes. We do not know whether these classes actually contained below average readers, but we do know that the pupils were not provided compensatory instruction, since there was none available in the school.

The 492 remaining teachers were in schools with compensatory programs. Even though they completed only the regular questionnaire, we decided to classify them as compensatory classes. This decision was based on the following considerations. All of these schools reported they had compensatory classes, but in many cases no compensatory questionnaires were completed. Given the distribution instructions, all of the teachers taught low average classes, and possibly even the worst classes in the school. It seems likely that special reading programs were in effect in these classrooms and that the principals and teachers were confused by the distribution instructions. Visual comparison of the data from this group and from the other identified compensatory classes showed no clear evidence of different patterns of responses.

The result of these classifications and sortings was the creation of two primary files: one contained 1926 compensatory teacher-class records; the second contained 106 regular teacher-class records.

Equating Compensatory and Regular Questionnaires

For our purposes in reanalysis, it made sense to treat the compensatory and regular questionnaires as equivalent forms. Most of the questions were in fact identical, and we handled the exceptions in the following ways (Table 1-6):

The regular questionnaire did not ask the teacher for the grade of the class. The grade was therefore estimated from the ages of the students in the class.

Where items were listed on one questionnaire but not the other, the data were treated as "missing."

Adjustments were carried out for a few items where the scales differed between the two questionnaires.

With these correspondences, we were able to treat all records as though the questionnaires were equivalent, which greatly simplified the reanalysis.

Abnormal Class Sizes

Examination of responses to the class-size question revealed an extraordinary range of answers. Some classes were reported to contain a single student, and other classes were as large as 600 students. We considered classes of less than 11 or more than 51 as questionable, requiring further investigation. A total of 134 classes fell outside these bounds.

In a number of these extreme cases, the response was corrected by using an alternate item; the teacher was asked on one item for class size, and on another item for reading class size. Thirty-eight records were corrected in this manner. In most of the remaining cases, other information in the record suggested that the teacher was actually a special educa-

Table 1-6
Differences between Compensatory and Regular Forms

Items	Compensatory	Regular
1 = Grade	Yes	No item - estimated
3a= No. of classes	Yes	No item - missing
7 = Race	None, 1-25%, 26-50% 51-75%, 76-100%	1-10%, 11-50%, 51-90%, 91-100%
9 = Pupil problems	None, 1-10%, 11-50% 51-100%, Don't know	None, 1-10%, 11-50% 51-90%, 91-100%, Don't know
pre 17 = No. of classes	Yes	No item - missing
pre 17 = No. of programs	Yes	No item - missing
17 = Time for reading	Yes	No item - missing
18 = Reduced subject area instruction	Yes	No item - missing
42 = Reading goals sub-item "visual discrimination"	No item - missing	Yes

tion teacher, who was handling several small tutorial groups. Ninety-six records of this sort were withdrawn from the data set.

Seventeen other classes were dropped because the majority of the questions were not answered.

The attrition rate from the screening described above was slight, 113 records (5%) were lost, leaving a total of 1919 records for the reanalysis. Several other minor editing changes were performed to achieve the highest possible accuracy. Some teachers had reversed the youngest and oldest age entries. When birth dates were reported these were transformed to age equivalents, using April 1972, the date of the survey—we had found a few records reporting 65-year-old elementary pupils!

The distribution of the records in the corrected file is shown in Table 1-7. The number of regular teachers is relatively small, which further supports our decision to make no attempt at a detailed analysis of these classes.

Table 1-7
Distribution of Schools and Teachers in Corrected Data File

386 Compensatory Schools (4.8 Teachers per School)		
2nd grade teachers	664	36%
4th grade teachers	630	34%
6th grade teachers	456	25%
Ungraded teachers	83	5%
Total	1833	

37 Regular Schools (2.3 Teachers per School)		
2nd grade teachers	33	38%
4th grade teachers	30	35%
6th grade teachers	22	26%
Ungraded teachers	1	1%
Total	86	

Organization of the Book

The survey data offer the opportunity for enlightenment on a number of complex issues. The task of examining and interpreting the data has been shared by a number of authors. It will be helpful to look in overview at the problems discussed in the rest of the book, and to indicate the specific tasks undertaken by each author.

Part I—The School and the Participants

The book is divided into four parts. The first part examines the characteristics of the schools, teachers, and pupils in compensatory reading classes as these are related to the stratifying variables—community size and income, percent minority enrollment, geographic region of the country, and size of the school, among others.

Allington looks at the communities and the schools within the communities in Chapter 2. The results are reasonable for the most part. Large schools are likely to have more compensatory programs than small schools. Busing is most prevalent in rural schools. Average income, variation in occupation, and rate of unemployment all affect principals' and teachers' attitudes toward their schools; they tend to be less satisfied in lower-income neighborhoods. There are few differences by region or by community size.

In Chapter 3, Sawyer presents a profile of the children who are in compensatory reading programs. The reasons for placing students in these programs—low achievement, teacher recommendation, disadvantagement—are discussed. The families of these children, their income, their occupations, and their racial origins, represent all levels and types within American society. However, students from lower income levels and those who move from school to school tend to be more frequently represented in the compensatory programs. The source cited most often for student problems is the same one mentioned by the principals in *The First R* study—the home environment.

Who teaches in compensatory programs? Harste and Strickler look at the training and experience of the teachers in Chapter 4. Most are experienced teachers with at least a bachelor's degree and a regular teaching certificate. Over half of the teachers have had some special training in reading, though how much and what kind of training is not specified. Harste and Strickler report that few of the compensatory reading teachers have met the International Reading Association's recommended standards. Children who have had difficulty in learning to read need the best professional assistance available. The question remains, have their teachers had the help they require in order to aid students?

Part II—Compensatory Reading Instruction

The second part of the book describes the compensatory programs offered within the schools. What is done for children having problems in learning to read? How do these special programs differ from regular programs? As noted above, there is no adequate comparison for instruction, the goals and activities of instruction, and the selection of materials. The survey allows us to describe what is being done for children whose performance has fallen below expected standards.

In Chapter 5, Pikulski and Kirsch outline the organization for compensatory instruction. They find that classroom organization of reading groups has changed little in the past decade. They report on the average amount of time for compensatory reading, the personnel for instruction, the number of teacher aides, volunteers, counselors, and reading specialists.

In Chapter 6, Howlett and Weintraub provide an overview of instructional procedures: the major goals, the instructional approaches used, and the time spent on various reading activities by these compensatory teachers. In all categories there are major differences from one grade to another; one does not teach compensatory reading in the same fashion to sixth-graders as to second-graders. Teachers who report using only one major approach to reading—basal, phonics, language experience, or individualized —differ in certain instructional goals and activities, but teachers vary more within an approach than between approaches.

Who selects the materials for reading instruction? This topic is covered by Dixon in Chapter 7. Although many teachers do not have a vote in the selection of instructional materials, both they and the principals indicate satisfaction with the materials being used. The results also show that compensatory teachers report using a wide variety of materials, very likely because supplemental funds make it possible to purchase supplemental materials.

Part III—Teacher Response Patterns and Predictions

The last part reexamines the responses of the teachers, but this time we look for structure in the multitude of responses on the class and program questionnaires. What patterns of response can be found? Are the patterns predictable by experience, training, or other factors? How are reading goals and practices determined by the grade level? The class size?

In Chapter 8, Drum and Calfee describe the procedures used in clustering the 260 separate responses on the teacher questionnaire. Factor analytic techniques were used to establish the composite scores on teacher attitudes, their reading goals, their instructional activities, and their feelings of success. The chapter explores the nature of the composite scores, the relationships among them, and differences by region, by grade level, by teacher experience, and by belief in compensatory programs.

Calfee and Drum examine in Chapter 9 the predictability of summary measures derived from the composites. We see there the importance of experience; teachers have different goals and spend time differently after they have taught for some years. The measures also depend greatly on the grade being taught, as one might expect. Of special interest are the strong relations between goals and plans for allocating time in reading. There are clear patterns to the teachers' responses to this survey, and the patterns have significant implications for the classroom.

Part IV—Summary

In Chapter 10, Drum and Calfee look back over the findings of the preceding chapters, with an eye to common themes and practical implications. The findings are related to other surveys of compensatory reading, and to *The First R*. There have been changes over the past decade—for instance, more books, more equipment, and more materials. Teachers are more likely to have had some special training. However, instructional practices are remarkably similar to those described in *The First R*.

The constancy of practice over time may reflect the wisdom and practicality of these practices. It may reveal inertia and resistance to change. It may result from reliance on money rather than on retraining and restructuring of the school as an organizational unit. The data do not permit choice among these and other explanations. What can be seen fairly clearly is that teachers differ widely in their goals in reading instruction and that their intended practices in the classroom are fairly consistent with these goals. Data from the later phases of the ETS survey will hopefully provide some insight into the relative effectiveness of teachers with different goals and practices. Whatever the outcome of these future analyses, we suspect that, where a teacher is ineffective in helping students to achieve success, changing the teacher's goals will be an essential step in changing practices.

Chapter 2

Communities and Schools

Richard L. Allington
State University of New York at Albany

The goal of this chapter is to describe the communities and the schools in which compensatory reading instruction has been implemented. At several points, schools with compensatory reading programs will be compared to schools without compensatory reading programs. The reader should remember that, in this survey, schools *without* compensatory reading programs are underrepresented in relation to their actual incidence in American education. The nonresponse rate in schools without compensatory programs was quite high, and as noted earlier, several other factors make the comparisons a bit tenuous. Nonetheless, the data do offer limited insights into certain features of schools, classes, and communities that do and do not have compensatory programs.

In the first section of this chapter, community characteristics are reported, with breakdown by community type and geographical region. The second section presents school characteristics and explores selected relationships between school and community variables. Of particular interest are the data on principals' satisfaction with their schools.

Community Characteristics

Several aspects of the community are described by responses to the School Principal Questionnaire. These have been sorted into two main categories. First is the community socioeconomic status, based on annual family income, rate of public assistance, occupational status, and educational attainment. The second category is community mobility and busing patterns. In this category, we also consider the racial-ethnic composition of the community.

These data provide useful demographic information about the communities in which the participating schools were located. However, the reader should be mindful that most of the data reflect the principals' estimates.

Socioeconomic Characteristics

Community socioeconomic status is most directly indicated by family income level. Other indicators from the principals' questionnaire include the number of families receiving public assistance, level of educational attainment, and ethnic background.

Family income. The principals' estimates of family income are shown in Table 2-1. About five percent of the principals reported extreme poverty (the majority of students from homes with annual incomes under $3,000). Twice this number said that most students were from homes with incomes above $12,000. Principals in schools with compensatory programs reported a mean annual family income around $8,500. The median family income in 1971 was about $10,037; the median was $10,672 for whites and $6,440 for blacks. The poverty level was placed at $4,137 for a nonfarm family of four (U.S. Department of Commerce, 1975a). To the degree that the principals' estimates were accurate, the family income in their communities was almost $2,000 below the national average. In schools without compensatory programs, the estimated income was actually a bit lower, with a mean of $8,000. However, the estimates were also more variable and less consistent. For instance, the percentages reported by principals with compensatory programs add up to 100 percent; the percentages by the other principals add up to 110 percent. We suspect that principals in poverty neighborhoods may have been more knowledgeable about community economic conditions.

An examination of the responses by community type (Table 2-1) confirms what one would expect from government statistics (U.S. Department of Commerce, 1975a) which show median income in suburbs at $11,287, in urban areas at $9,150, and in rural areas at $7,928. The principals' estimate of income for schools with compensatory programs was highest in suburban ($8,600) and urban ($8,200) communities, lowest in rural areas ($7,700). As mentioned earlier, we question the accuracy of the reports from other schools.

Estimates of the percentage of families receiving public assistance is another indicator of socioeconomic status of the community. About half the principals reported that less than ten percent of the families received public assistance. Another third indicated that between 11 and 25 percent of the families received assistance. Generally speaking, the data show more families on public assistance in schools with compensatory programs than in schools without such programs, especially in rural and urban communities.

The data on family income and public assistance in different geographic regions present few surprises, except for the size of the discrepancy between the Southeastern United States and the rest of the country. Principals in Southern schools estimated annual family income at $7,100, compared to $8,700 in other regions. These estimates follow the pattern

Table 2-1
Principal Estimates of Percentage of Families at Selected Income Levels
and Percentage Receiving Public Assistance. Mean (and Standard Deviation)

	Over $12000	$11999 to 9000	$8999 to 6000	$5999 to 3000	$2999 and Below	Receive Public Assistance	Number
Compensatory Programs	18 (21)	23 (19)	28 (22)	22 (21)	11 (16)	17 (18)	348
Community							
Urban	18 (22)	23 (20)	25 (21)	22 (19)	14 (19)	20 (21)	74
Suburban	20 (22)	24 (19)	30 (22)	20 (20)	9 (12)	14 (17)	155
Rural	14 (17)	22 (18)	28 (22)	25 (23)	13 (19)	19 (18)	119
Region							
Northeast	21 (23)	24 (18)	32 (21)	18 (16)	8 (10)	15 (18)	77
North Central	18 (20)	26 (19)	29 (23)	20 (22)	9 (12)	14 (16)	127
Southeastern	13 (17)	17 (16)	25 (19)	30 (23)	19 (22)	24 (21)	110
Western	20 (22)	26 (19)	30 (22)	18 (17)	9 (13)	15 (15)	71
No Compensatory Programs	16 (24)	23 (17)	32 (22)	27 (28)	10 (14)	13 (17)	34

reported by the Department of Commerce (1977). The percentage of families on public assistance in the South was estimated at 25 percent; elsewhere the estimate was 15 percent.

Family occupation. Principals' estimates of family occupations are shown in Table 2-2. There is little difference between schools with and without compensatory programs. The general pattern is that higher occupational status is found in urban and suburban communities, and in the Northeastern and Western regions. These results are generally parallel to those for family income, with the exception of the somewhat lower job status of families in the North Central region. However, unemployment is estimated to be lowest in this region, which has the highest rate of families headed by skilled workers. The overall picture for these schools is a high proportion of skilled, white collar and unskilled workers. Unemployment tends to be slightly higher in urban areas and in the Southeastern states, but at the time of this survey principals believed that most families had a working breadwinner.

Educational attainment. Each principal was asked to estimate the educational attainment of the students' families (Table 2-3). The scale for responding to this question was not very finely graded, and the estimates were accordingly rough. Estimates by principals without compensatory programs were especially variable and inconsistent.

We urge caution in interpreting the results in Table 2-3. We suspect that, because it is their life's endeavor, educators may overestimate the educational achievement of their students' parents. Actually, the number of citizens who have not completed high school still outnumbers the college graduates in the total population, and a small but fairly substantial number of students come from homes in which the household head did not attend high school (U.S. Department of Commerce, 1974).

Generally speaking, the principals' estimates reflect a high level of educational attainment. Only a few principals (13 percent) reported as many as one out of ten of the students from homes in which the head of the household had not completed the eighth grade. More than one in five families was estimated to have a head of household with some college training. These estimates are somewhat higher than the National Center for Educational Statistics (NCES) report. The proportion of high school graduates has remained constant since 1962—at about 70 percent (NCES, 1975).

Rural communities have slightly lower levels of educational attainment than urban or suburban communities, which are about the same. More rural families are estimated to have completed only elementary school, and fewer to have had any college. Breakdown of educational attainment by region shows again the Southeastern states were behind other regions in 1972. Less than half the families were estimated to have completed high school, compared to more than two-thirds of the families

Table 2-2
Principal Estimates of Job Status of Student Families. Mean (and Standard Deviation)

	Professional	Business	White Collar	Skilled	Unskilled	Unemployed	Number
Compensatory Programs	9 (11)	12 (13)	24 (18)	27 (21)	24 (23)	10 (12)	385
Community							
Urban	10 (12)	12 (13)	26 (18)	26 (21)	23 (21)	12 (14)	74
Suburban	11 (13)	14 (14)	26 (17)	25 (18)	22 (21)	9 (11)	155
Rural	7 (6)	10 (11)	20 (16)	29 (22)	27 (24)	11 (12)	119
Region							
Northeastern	10 (13)	13 (13)	29 (19)	24 (17)	22 (22)	10 (13)	77
North Central	8 (9)	11 (13)	23 (17)	30 (23)	22 (22)	8 (10)	127
Southeastern	8 (10)	11 (13)	19 (14)	25 (22)	31 (24)	13 (14)	110
Western	10 (12)	14 (12)	29 (20)	26 (17)	19 (18)	11 (11)	71
No Compensatory Program	9 (13)	12 (11)	24 (18)	29 (20)	19 (17)	8 (12)	37

Communities and Schools

Table 2-3

Principal Estimates of Percentage of Families Attaining Selected
Levels of Education. Mean (and Standard Deviation)

	Attended College	Graduated High School	Only Attended High School	Graduated Grade 8	Only Attended Elementary	Number
Compensatory Programs	20 (19)	43 (24)	21 (19)	14 (19)	9 (12)	348
Community						
Urban	21 (23)	42 (25)	22 (20)	13 (19)	8 (12)	74
Suburban	21 (20)	44 (23)	18 (19)	13 (20)	6 (8)	155
Rural	15 (16)	42 (24)	23 (17)	14 (18)	11 (15)	119
Region						
Northeastern	23 (20)	50 (25)	17 (14)	10 (12)	6 (6)	77
North Central	19 (19)	46 (23)	19 (17)	11 (17)	7 (10)	127
Southeastern	17 (19)	35 (21)	26 (19)	19 (24)	14 (17)	110
Western	19 (19)	44 (25)	21 (23)	14 (21)	7 (8)	71
No Compensatory Programs	20 (22)	47 (25)	27 (24)	16 (24)	10 (17)	34

elsewhere in the nation. A supporting trend is noted in the National Assessment of Educational Progress report that young adults in the Southeast had the lowest performance of all regions on several measures of reading areas (NAEP, 1976).

Racial-ethnic makeup. Next we look at the racial-ethnic composition of the communities as estimated by the principals (Table 2-4). There is no necessary reason why the proportion of minority students in a community should be related to the socioeconomic status, but the correlation between these two variables remains substantial at the present time, reflecting in part the nation's heritage. Most principals reported that about 90 percent of the student population was Caucasian. About 10 percent indicated a majority enrollment of Black students, and about the same number responded that more than one out of ten had a Spanish surname. Relatively few principals reported a significant Oriental or Native American enrollment.

Table 2-4 displays the principals' estimates of students from different racial-ethnic backgrounds by program, community, and region. Urban schools, compensatory programs, and the Western and Southern regions had the greatest proportion of minority residents, as one might expect.

Mobility

Census data indicate that Americans are quite mobile—41 percent of the population move at least once every five years (U.S. Department of Commerce, 1975b). The mobility rate for young adults is over 60 percent, and one would expect the rate to be higher for elementary school children than for secondary students. Educational attainment also affects mobility. People with college degrees are more likely to change residence than those without such degrees. The South and West have greater numbers of persons moving into their regions than moving out, while the other regions reverse this trend.

Student moving. Principals were asked to estimate the percentage of students moving into and out of the school during the school year and the percentage of migrant students. The data in Table 2-5 summarize these estimates. Over two-thirds of principals said that less than 10 percent of the students moved into or out of the school attendance area during the year. About a quarter of the principals reported somewhat more shifting about of students, and in a few schools student mobility was substantial.

There were no noticeable differences in mobility between schools with and without compensatory reading programs. However, urban schools had 50 percent higher mobility than suburban or rural schools. This pattern is supported by other data (U.S. Department of Commerce, 1975c). The distribution of responses by geographic region reveals that mobility was more substantial in the West than in other regions, again as one would expect from census data.

Table 2-4

Principal Estimates of Percentage of Students from Selected Racial-Ethnic Backgrounds
Mean (and Standard Deviation)

	Caucasian	Black	Spanish	Oriental[a]	Native American[a]	Other	Number
Compensatory Programs	74 (30)	18 (25)	8 (11)	4 (2)	5 (3)	1 (5)	385
Community							
Urban	64 (36)	25 (30)	11 (18)	5 (3)	4 (2)	1 (2)	74
Suburban	79 (25)	14 (20)	7 (8)	5 (3)	5 (4)	2 (8)	155
Rural	74 (28)	19 (24)	7 (9)	4 (2)	4 (2)	1 (2)	119
Region							
Northeastern	81 (27)	16 (26)	5 (4)	4 (2)	4 (2)	1 (2)	77
North Central	81 (27)	14 (24)	5 (5)	5 (1)	5 (1)	1 (2)	127
Southeastern	63 (31)	30 (26)	6 (8)	4 (2)	4 (2)	1 (2)	110
Western	71 (30)	12 (19)	17 (20)	5 (4)	5 (5)	3 (12)	71
No Compensatory Programs	83 (20)	12 (15)	8 (15)	4 (2)	5 (5)	3 (16)	37

[a]The response scale was coarse and did not permit fine distinctions

Table 2-5
Principal Estimates of Percentage of Student Mobility and Migrant Students. Mean (and Standard Deviation)

	Percent Moving In		Percent Moving Out		Percent Migrants		Number
Compensatory Programs	12	(14)	11	(15)	6	(6)	339
Community							
Urban	15	(16)	15	(16)	6	(4)	72
Suburban	11	(10)	11	(11)	7	(9)	150
Rural	11	(10)	9	(9)	6	(2)	117
Region							
Northeastern	9	(6)	8	(6)	6	(4)	74
North Central	10	(11)	10	(12)	6	(4)	126
Southeastern	11	(12)	10	(11)	6	(5)	105
Western	17	(13)	16	(14)	7	(11)	70
No Compensatory Programs	13	(12)	12	(12)	5	(0)	34

Data on migrant families are also reported in Table 2-5. These families present special problems of mobility. The seasonal nature of their employment dictates a high level of mobility as the migrant worker follows the crop harvests within and across geographical regions. Children of migrant workers seldom obtain a formal education, due to the transient lifestyle and the economic necessity of children working with the family. Recent surveys indicate that less than 10 percent of migrant children finish high school, and the median educational attainment level of migrant workers is about fourth grade (U.S. Comptroller General, 1973). This situation persists despite continuing efforts by federal agents to improve the lot of these students, largely because the migrant student is truly mobile—often remaining in a school attendance area for less than one month. This instability, when coupled with social, cultural, and language differences between home and school, produces an educational dilemma for which an effective answer remains to be found.

An examination of the principals' estimates of the incidence of migrant students reveals that the number of schools in this sample enrolling these children was quite limited. A few schools (12) reported that migrant students accounted for as much as a quarter of the enrollment, and in some schools (7) half the students were from migrant worker families. Neither community type nor geographical region was related to these estimates. Unfortunately, the questionnaire did not provide a "0 percent" category, and so the responses were not very precise.

Busing. Related to mobility is the extent to which students are bused outside neighborhood attendance areas. Principals were asked to indicate whether there was *any* busing of students into or outside of neighborhood areas and *if* there was any busing, what percentage of students were bused. The data on these two questions are shown in Table 2-6. One point should be kept in mind in looking at these data—some principals who said that there was no busing then proceeded to report the percentage of students bused! It appears that these individuals did not notice that they were to give a percentage estimate only if there was some busing. We suspect that the percentages of students bused reported in the table may be *low* by 10 to 20 percent.

About one-third of the principals reported busing for some purpose in their schools. In about 20 percent of the schools, more than half of the students were bused. The percentage of schools with busing is slightly higher in rural areas than elsewhere. These figures apply to schools with compensatory programs. For schools without any such programs, the

Table 2-6

Busing in Schools as a Function of Program, Community, and Region

	Schools with Busing		% Students Bused in Schools with Busing		
	%	n[a]	m	s.d.	n[b]
Compensatory Programs	29	384	26	25	215
Community Type					
Urban	28	74	23	24	42
Suburban	27	154	24	24	80
Rural	32	119	29	24	69
Region					
Northeast	14	77	37	28	38
North Central	27	127	21	24	63
South	39	109	28	23	69
West	34	71	20	22	45
No Compensatory Programs	12	37	30	27	13

Note a - Total number of schools in category

Note b - Number of schools in category with estimate of busing

amount of busing was much less, generally half that reported for schools with compensatory programs. Principals reported more busing in Southern and Western schools, but the number of students in a school who were affected by busing was greatest in the Northeast.

Busing takes time from the students' school day and creates disruption in the relation between student, parent, neighborhood, and school. We are not questioning whether busing is right or wrong; concerns other than the student's educational stability have led to increased busing. However, it should be emphasized that the teachers described in this report were responsible for developing and carrying out instructional programs to help students who were from poverty backgrounds, whose academic achievement was generally poor, and who were also moved daily to a school setting distant from their neighborhood and family. Such conditions would pose a continuing challenge to any teacher.

School Characteristics

This section describes information from the principals' questionnaire about schools with compensatory programs, including data on enrollments, per pupil expenditures, and incidence of reading deficiency. Next we look at the principals' judgments about satisfaction with the physical plant, personnel, and materials, and we compare these judgments with the teachers' responses to similar questions.

School Enrollment

In Table 2-7 are data on the size of the school. Mean student enrollment was slightly more than six hundred pupils. Ninety percent of the schools enrolled between 150 and 650 students. This result fits well with the finding that most students in the United States attend schools with enrollments between 300 and 700 located in districts that have between 1200 and 25,000 students in grades K-12 (NCES, 1976). Less than 3 percent of the sample had fewer than a hundred students, reflecting the demise of the small neighborhood school and the small rural school. While small schools are increasingly less common, they have not quite vanished from the educational picture. Recent data (NCES, 1976) indicate that a third of all school districts in this country had K-12 enrollments of fewer than 300 students. On the other hand, an indicator of the trend to larger schools is the finding that the 100,000 schools operating in the United States today are about half the number operating in 1945 (NIE, 1976).

Another index of school size is the number of classrooms. A single principal in the sample said that he oversaw a one-room school; in contrast, the largest school had more than sixty classrooms. On the average, the six hundred students in the typical school were housed in a building with twenty-one classrooms.

Table 2-7
School Enrollment. Mean (and Standard Deviation)

	Enrollment		n
Compensatory Programs	624	(222)	385
Community			
Urban	712	(208)	74
Suburban	626	(207)	155
Rural	577	(223)	119
Region			
Northeast	661	(227)	77
North Central	585	(238)	127
South	631	(229)	110
West	645	(165)	71
No Compensatory Programs	616	(274)	37

As might be expected, urban schools were largest, followed by suburban and then rural schools (Table 2-7). On the average, an urban school had about 25 percent more students than a rural school, but there was considerable variability within the community types. The collapsing of urbanization categories from nine to three may have obscured some systematic trends, to be sure. Regional variations were negligible. Schools without compensatory reading programs tended to have slightly smaller enrollments, but the difference was neither statistically nor practically significant.

Several other variables were examined for their relationship with school enrollment. Minority student population was positively related to enrollment; as school size increased, so did the percentage of minority students. In part, this is because large schools and minority concentration were both typical of urban areas. On the other hand, Coleman's (1975) analysis of integration patterns showed a drop in the number of segregated schools, with small, Southern districts leading the way. Larger districts in the Northeast, North Central, and Western regions have been more resistant to integration. These changes would appear partly responsible for the present relation between school size and minority percentage.

Busing of students was positively related to school size. Larger schools also tended to have students from lower family income levels, though the relationship was negligible at the lowest level (less than $3,000). Families with this income level were equally often reported in urban and rural areas, in large and small schools.

Expenditure per Pupil

The principal questionnaire included several items on per pupil expenditure. The principal was asked about the school's total expenditure per pupil for the preceding year, and the expenditure per pupil for the compensatory reading program. Over half of the principals did not answer the question. We believe that the data from those who did respond must be viewed with caution, because of self-selection and response bias. There is no guarantee about the accuracy of responses—a few extreme estimates are especially questionable. Previous analysis of these data revealed a lack of agreement about expenditures between the responses of chief school district officers and principal (Rubin, et al., 1973). Because of such concerns about the quality of the data, no detailed breakdown will be attempted—the descriptive statistics reported should be taken with a grain of salt.

The mean expenditure per pupil in this survey was $626. Twenty percent of the principals said the total expenditure per student was less than $200, ten percent said it was greater than $1,000. The compensatory expenditure was $293 per student. However, the distribution was sharply skewed, over 60 percent of the respondents reported a contribution of less than $200 per student from the compensatory program.

These figures would have been more meaningful if we knew the extent to which the compensatory expenditures were over and above some base rate. The data were not available, nor is this volume the place for a complete examination of this matter. However, there are certain signs that compensatory funds were not always used for supplementation, but in some instances served only to supplant regular costs. For instance, there was only a $66 difference between pupil expenditures in Title I and non-Title I schools—principals in Title I schools reported spending less. Analysis of compensatory expenditures showed that schools with Title I and other sources of funding spent an average of $308, while total Title I only and non-Title I programs spent about $180. Schools with Title I plus other funding were receiving other sources of revenue, so it is not surprising that compensatory expenditures per pupil should have been higher in these schools, which also reported fewer students in compensatory reading programs. These programs appear to have concentrated primarily on students with serious reading deficiencies, which may have permitted instruction that was more intense, with smaller groups working longer periods of time.

We should also mention that since 1972, the time of this survey, the auditing of Title I programs has been substantially tightened up, to ensure that funds serve to augment rather than supplant. For instance, the NIE study of allocation of Title I funds further shows that this support is presently reaching schools in communities where economic need is greatest, as intended by the framers of the 1965 legislation (NIE, 1977).

Expenditure per pupil is closely related to the socioeconomic status of the community (Figure 2-1). The dilemma of schools in low-income neighborhoods is portrayed in the figure. Most of them spend relatively little money for educating a student. Schools in higher income communities are far more likely to spend a lot of money per student. They can generally support these greater expenditures at relatively small cost in percentage of family income. Families in low-income neighborhoods spend a relatively high proportion of their income on education, but still spend considerably less per student than do high-income communities (Coons, Clune, & Sugarman, 1970; Odden et al., 1976). Past efforts of state governments to equalize financing in the public schools have remedied the situation somewhat (Wise, 1968) and responses to the Serrano-Priest decision are increasing pressures on states to achieve equity (Chaffee, 1977; McDermott, 1977). The extent of inequity at the national level *in compensatory schools* was substantial at the time of this survey, and seems likely to still be of considerable magnitude.

When the survey data were examined by geographic region and community type, the major conclusion was that suburban schools had higher per pupil expenditures than either urban or rural schools, regardless of region. Schools in the Northeast and North Central regions generally had the highest per pupil expenditures, followed by the West and South, respectively. In some instances, the differences between mean expenditures for the same community types were very substantial. For instance, the Northeast or North Central average was more than twice that of the South.

The issues surrounding per pupil expenditures are important but hard to group. Education costs are rising faster than the cost of living; they doubled between 1961 and 1971 (Grant, 1972). Critics complain that benefits are decreasing; academic achievement has assuredly declined over the past decade (Armbruster, 1977). Finally, there are the complexities of the variable costs of educating different kinds of children in different communities and geographic regions.

This study was not designed to permit a cost-benefit analysis; neither the character of the questions nor the low response rate by the principals engenders much confidence in the results. Nonetheless, the results do depict levels and patterns of expenditures. Especially interesting is the

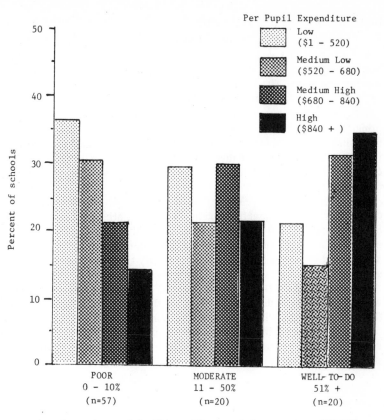

Figure 2-1. Relation between family income in community and total school expenditure per pupil

finding that, even within schools with compensatory programs, the typical pattern is for higher expenditures per student in higher-income communities.

Our primary focus in this book has been the role of the teacher in compensatory programs. The effect of additional funds should be to provide for additional classroom resources—people, materials, training, and so on. The data suggest that principals were not generally aware of the marginal impact of additional funds. We would be curious to know the *teachers'* perceptions about the impact of supplementary funds to obtain additional resources.

Incidence of Reading Deficiency

The principal questionnaire asked for an "estimate [of] the percentage of students in your school at each of the following grade levels [2, 4, and 6] who are reading one or more years below grade level according to current test data. The estimate should be based upon the concept of national norms for the grade for which you are reporting."

Figure 2-2 depicts the major features of the principals' responses. The principals reported that increasing numbers of students at the later grades had fallen behind expected levels of performance. A third of the principals thought that only a few of their second-graders were in difficulty. Only a quarter of the principals believed that most of their sixth-graders were doing well.

In Table 2-8 the principals' estimates are displayed by program, community, and geographic region. Suburban principals and those in Southern and Western schools reported a slightly lower incidence of reading deficiency, but the trend for increasing deficiency with rising grade levels stood up across schools in all community types and regions. There is also evidence in the table that principals were less sure of the situation in the later grades. Of the 356 compensatory program principals who were willing to estimate the reading level of their second-graders, only 305 (86 percent) were willing to give the same estimate for sixth-graders.

We investigated the relation between principals' estimates of expenditures and reading failure. The comparison was made for fourth grade students in schools with Title I and other funds. Figure 2-3 presents the

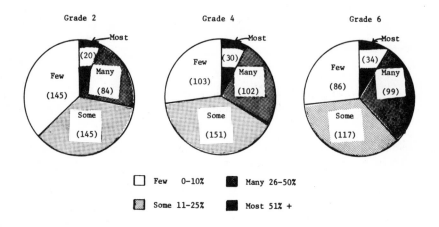

Figure 2.2 Principal estimates of percentage of students at grades 2, 4 and 6 one or more years behind in reading. Number in parentheses is number of principals reporting in a category.

Table 2-8
Principal Estimates of Percentage of Students
at Grades 2, 4, and 6 One or More Years Behind in Reading

	Grade 2			Grade 4			Grade 6		
	m	s.d.	n	m	s.d.	n	m	s.d.	n
Compensatory Programs	18	(17)	356	22	(18)	350	24	(19)	305
Community									
Urban	23	(20)	70	23	(19)	68	25	(20)	64
Suburban	16	(15)	140	21	(19)	141	20	(17)	124
Rural	20	(18)	112	24	(19)	107	27	(22)	89
Region									
Northeast	16	(14)	72	18	(17)	68	20	(18)	52
North Central	14	(11)	119	18	(17)	122	20	(14)	111
South	26	(22)	97	29	(22)	93	30	(22)	77
West	20	(16)	68	23	(18)	67	25	(21)	65
No Compensatory Programs	16	(16)	37	21	(14)	35	25	(19)	30

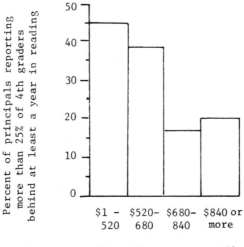

Expenditures per pupil

*Figure 2-3. Relation between expenditures per
pupil and principals' judgment of
need for compensatory reading
instruction.*

Communities and Schools

results. As can be seen, the trend is for schools with lower per pupil expenditures to exhibit higher levels of student failure, at least by the principals' estimate. This finding accords with earlier results showing a slight but noticeable link between funding and achievement (HEW, 1972; however, cf. Coleman, 1966).

Principals' and Teachers' Evaluation of the School

Principals were asked to evaluate their schools on a variety of characteristics, including physical plant, instructional staff, and materials. Teachers were also asked how they felt about some of these matters, and we will compare their responses with the principals' judgments.

Mayeske et al. (1969) concluded that school personnel were more strongly involved with school outcomes than with physical facilities, programs, policies, and the like. One hears reports that the school staff feels that all characteristics of the learning environment are interrelated, if only in a small way, to the overall effectiveness of the school. For instance, the adequacy of the school facilities is an indication of comunity interest and support of education. By contrast, some surveys have shown that satisfaction with school facilities is not strongly related to levels of school achievement (NYSED, 1976).

The relevant items on the principal and teacher questionnaires are displayed in Table 2-9, together with the average ratings. The correspondence between principal and teacher ratings is rough at best. We see that both groups tended to respond with a qualified "OK" to most categories. Principals were slightly less satisfied than teachers; they wanted more staff (though not more teachers) and more audiovisual materials. Teachers were generally happy with their colleagues, with the administration, and with the philosophy of the school. Students were their only source of dissatisfaction, more particularly student attitudes. Principals were not asked about the quality of the staff, only about the number of staff. Neither were they asked what they thought about the students. Similarly, teachers were asked only about the "faculty in general"—they were not asked whether they thought the staff was big enough to maintain adequate student-teacher ratios. The principals did not see a problem in student-teacher ratios, but they did want more paraprofessionals, who are considerably less expensive than teachers.

It would be enlightening to discover what duties the principals would assign the paraprofessionals. The ratings might be interpreted as indicating the principals' feeling that the instructional staff could handle the job if additional paraprofessionals were available to take care of noninstructional tasks. On the other hand, some schools have seen a disturbing trend to use paraprofessionals to supplant professional instructional personnel, particularly in the delivery of tutorial assistance (Conant, 1973). Unfortunately,

Table 2-9
Principal and Teacher Ratings of Satisfaction on
Selected Aspects of School. Rating Scales Were:
1 - Highly adequate (or satisfied)
2 - Adequate (or moderately satisfied)
3 - inadequate (or moderately dissatisfied)
4 - Highly Inadequate (or dissatisfied)

Principals' Questionnaire				Teachers' Questionnaire			
Category	m	s.d.	n	Category	m	s.d.	n
Personnel				Personnel			
Faculty	2.0	.6	422	Faculty	1.5	.6	1825
Other Personnel	2.3	.7	418	Administration	1.7	.8	1817
Teacher Aides	2.8	.8	415	Overall Philosophy	1.8	.7	1816
Nonprofessionals	2.4	.7	412				
Physical Plant				Physical Plant			
Size	2.0	.8	422	General	1.9	.8	1825
Condition	1.9	.7	422				
Suitability	2.1	.8	418				
Materials				Students			
Quantity of Books	1.9	.6	419	Ability	2.0	.7	1817
Quality of Books	1.9	.5	419	Attitudes	2.2	.8	1817
Quantity of AV	2.1	.7	418				
Quality of AV	1.9	.6	417				
Quantity of Equipment	2.1	.6	420				
Quality of Equipment	1.9	.5	419				

the data do not speak to the quality of paraprofessional assignment but only to principals' satisfaction with the number of personnel.

We looked for relations between the principals' ratings of satisfaction with the school and other selected factors—incidence of reading failure, expenditure per pupil, and family income level. Four specific items were selected for analysis: condition of the physical plant, number of instructional personnel, number of teacher aides, and quantity of books. For each of these items, the measure was the percentage of principals who answered that the situation in their school was either inadequate or highly inadequate.

First, the general trend in three of the four items was that the principal was satisfied if he estimated a low incidence of reading failure. The exception was the principals' judgment about the number of teacher aides; regardless of the incidence of reading failure, most principals felt they needed more aides.

Expenditure per pupil showed little relation to principal satisfaction, but this result largely reflects the low response rate of principals to cost questions. They were more likely to estimate family income in the community, and in this instance the relation was strong and positive. Principals in schools with a high proportion of middle-class families were relatively satisfied with the school facilities and staff—except for the number of teacher aides, of course.

The generally favorable evaluations indicate that most principals were satisfied with the status quo. In contrast, the Austin and Morrison report (1963) found administrators dissatisfied with instructional personnel, physical plants, number and suitability of books for students. The comparison suggests that American elementary schools have upgraded many visible facets of the educational process in the past decade, at least in compensatory classrooms. Part of this improvement in principal evaluations can be attributed to the dissemination of funds through the Elementary and Secondary Education Act (ESEA) program inaugurated in 1965, especially Title I of ESEA. The expenditures may have been small in relation to per pupil base support, but the "multiplier effect" has been significant in this instance (Halperin, 1975).

Summary

The past decade has seen a heightening of concern about social and educational factors which influence equal educational opportunity in American schools. Considerable time, effort, and money have been expended to identify institutional and pedagogical influences on achievement by low ability, disadvantaged, high risk students. The present study, like others before it, does not yield a complete understanding of the relation between community, school, and student performance. However, the survey has provided useful evidence about the community background in schools with compensatory programs, and about the relations between community and school characteristics.

The analysis of community characteristics in this chapter reveals the diversity of social environments from which American schools draw their students. Schools with compensatory programs serve communities with generally less advantaged families, according to the principals' judgments. Some schools had large concentrations of students from families with annual incomes of less than $4,000, families at or below the poverty level. In a few schools, most families received public assistance. However, most principals reported the typical family as being in the lower-middle income range, with annual incomes between $6,000 and $12,000.

At the time of this survey (1972), elementary schools reflected the racial-ethnic makeup of the community. Although nearly a quarter of the schools reported some busing of students in or out of the attendance area, the racial-ethnic composition of schools showed considerable evidence of imbalance, with heavy concentration of minority groups in certain schools. Student mobility was less than 10 percent in most schools, but was quite high in a few schools.

The principals' descriptions of the schools reflect the national pattern of schools with large enrollments and big facilities. The larger schools were typically found in urban neighborhoods and tended to have lower achievement scores on the average. School organization was predominantly along grade-level lines; ungraded classes were rare in compensatory programs.

The survey is disappointing in the cost data it provides. Many principals left blank the questions about sources of funding and expenditures. We cannot tell whether the low response rate was a matter of choice or lack of knowledge. The data that were available show a trend for schools in the relatively wealthier communities to spend more money per pupil and to have fewer students reading below grade level. Principals gave no clear evidence that federal and state compensatory funds were providing supplemental increments to the per pupil expenditures. The survey results are consistent with other data showing substantial disparities in per pupil expenditure from one locality to another.

Principals and teachers were asked about their satisfaction with several features of the educational environment. The principals were asked different questions than were the teachers, so direct comparison is not possible. However, both groups were generally satisfied with their colleagues and working conditions. Principals wanted more teacher aides, and teachers were unhappy with the students' ability and attitude. These positions may reflect the nature of the questions but may also be a fairly accurate reflection of concerns.

Chapter 3

A Profile of Children
In Compensatory Reading Programs

Diane J. Sawyer
Syracuse University

The Educational Testing Service study of compensatory reading programs in the United States provides descriptive information on the elementary students who participated in compensatory reading programs. Profiles of these children should serve a useful role in systematic program development for improving literacy.

Selection of Students for Compensatory Instruction

Poor Achievement

How does the school decide which students to place in a compensatory program? In about one out of five schools this was not an issue—the principal reported that *all* of the children in the school were in the program. Eighty-one percent of the principals said that children were selected for inclusion in compensatory reading classes because test results showed they were reading below grade level. These test results were backed up by teacher judgment according to 79 percent of the principals who said that pupil participation was also based on teacher recommendation. Thirty-eight percent of the principals indicated that students were in the program at the request of parents, and eight percent reported that individual pupils volunteered for the program.

Funding considerations also determined the selection of pupils. Over 29 percent of the principals reported that children were included in the program because they were members of specific target groups, like the economically disadvantaged, and Aid for Dependent Children families. To be sure, these children are also likely to be reading below the norm for the grade placement. Federal or state targeted compensatory programs often specify an achievement level of at least six months below grade placement for a student to qualify for inclusion.

Summer programs appear to use the same selection criteria. However, some effort is also made to include students in summer programs who have had no previous compensatory reading instruction, according to six percent of the principals surveyed.

Student Background

The rationale for inclusion of a student in a compensatory program has been frequently justified on the assumption of disadvantagement in the home. Principals were asked to estimate the percentage of students in compensatory programs from culturally, linguistically, or economically deprived backgrounds. The data show that for one in eight schools, the principal reported that at least 95 percent of the students were deprived. However, 70 percent of the principals reported that deprived students made up less than half the compensatory program. The picture that emerges is one in which disadvantaged students comprise a substantial proportion of the typical compensatory program, but by no means a majority. Students were in compensatory programs because of academic (and possibly behavioral) problems, not because of deprivation—at least this is what principals judged to be the case.

More recent evidence confirms certain features of this picture. For instance, one report claims that economically disadvantaged students are in the majority in only 25 percent of ESEA Title I schools (SDC, 1978). However, it is also true that 90 percent of the schools where poverty students are in the majority receive Title I funds. The Congressionally mandated study of Title I by NIE shows that, as of 1975, funds were being reasonably well allocated to schools with the highest proportion of poverty families *and,* in addition, that a substantial proportion (57 percent) of students in academic need were also being served (NIE, 1977).

Previous Experience in Compensatory Programs

The intent of compensatory instruction has been to help the student bring lagging skills "up to level." The chief method for achieving this goal has been intensive instruction, often in specialized out-of-class settings. The frequently voiced hope is that the student will attain a level of proficiency necessary to handle comfortably the reading requirements of the regular classroom. It is not uncommon, unfortunately, to find students remaining in compensatory programs year after year.

Teachers in the survey were asked to estimate the percentage of pupils in their compensatory classes who had been assigned to similar classes the prior year. The results in Table 3-1 show that, at successive grade levels, it is increasingly likely that the children have had prior experience in compensatory programs. This trend shows up most clearly in the

Table 3-1

Teachers' Estimates of Percent of Students
in Compensatory Programs prior to Survey Year

Teachers' Estimates of Percent	G R A D E			
	2nd (n=559)	4th (n=511)	6th (n=378)	Ungraded (n= 78)
Mean	37	46	50	37
(s.d.)	(39)	(39)	(39)	(33)
0%	22	8	7	14
1- 10%	34	35	32	31
25- 50%	10	16	14	23
50- 75%	8	7	9	17
75-100%	26	34	38	15

bottom line of the table, which shows the percentage of teachers who estimated that virtually all of their students had been in a compensatory program previously. This percentage increases from 26 percent at second grade to 38 percent at sixth grade. Thus it is common for children in compensatory reading instruction to have been included in such programs for two and possibly more years. At all grades, half the teachers reported that a substantial proportion of their students (35 percent or more) had come from previous compensatory programs.

Characteristics of Students in Compensatory Programs

Sex

For at least a generation, the popular assumption has been that boys experience more difficulty in learning to read. Teachers surveyed in this study reported that, on the average, about 57 percent of the students in their compensatory classes were boys. Teachers of ungraded compensatory reading classes reported that 63 percent of their students were boys. Boys do predominate in these classes, though not to the degree that would be expected from some previous research reports. For instance, Blom (1970) reported studies of reading disabilities with male-female ratios ranging from 57 percent boys to as high as 94 percent boys.

Age

The age ranges reported for children in compensatory reading classes are shown in Table 3-2. The data reveal one interesting feature. We suppose that the typical age range for entry to first grade is from five years, nine months to six years, eleven months. The survey was carried out in the spring of the year, which adds eight months to these numbers. This leads us to expect that the second-graders should range from seven years, five months to eight years, seven months. In second grade, the youngest children were about the age we would expect, but the oldest children were about six months older than expected. The data suggest noticeable retention of students in compensatory programs as early as second grade. More significantly, the youngest-oldest averages in the fourth grade were almost exactly two years more than the second grade averages, and the sixth grade averages exceeded by two years those for the fourth grade— just as one would predict. An inferential leap is required, but the data are consistent with the notion that there was a moderate degree of retention during the early grades for compensatory students, but from second grade onward, they were passed from one grade to the next without any substantial retention.

Preschool Experience

Since the 1950s, and particularly during the 1960s, the preschool movement has seen steady growth in the United States (Day & Parker, 1977; Evans, 1976). Kindergartens have become generally accepted components of public elementary school programs. Headstart, Day Care, and private preschool programs have become increasingly available to children from various economic backgrounds. During the latter half of the 1960s government-sponsored programs such as Headstart and Day Care were developed with the aim of intervention for enrichment of childhood experience. It was felt that many children failed in school because of inadequate preparation for demands of school learning and the preschool would develop language facility and learning competence, leading to greater chances of school success among the disadvantaged (Deutsch, 1967).

Teachers in the ETS survey were asked to estimate the percent of children in their classes who had attended some form of preschool, excluding kindergarten. Average percentages in Table 3-3 decrease over grades, which may reflect the growth in federally sponsored day care and preschool programs. Sixth grade pupils at the time of the survey would have been eligible for preschool programs in 1963 and 1964. Second-graders would have attended during 1967 and 1968. By the end of the decade of the 1960s, preschools had become more commonplace. The data suggest that with each decrease in grade, more and more parents were taking advantage of such programs. Of course, it is also conceivable

Table 3-2

Average Age Ranges of Students in Compensatory Reading Programs

| | 2nd (n=601) | | 4th (n=567) | | 6th (n=418) | | Ungraded (n=81) | |
	Average Years/ Months	s.d.	Average Years/ Months	s.d.	Average Years/ Months	s.d.	Average Years/ Months	s.d.
Age of Youngest Student	7/7	(5)	9/6	(8)	11/4	(9)	7/10	(18)
Age of Oldest Student	9/1	(8)	11/3	(10)	13/4	(10)	12/4	(19)

Table 3-3
Teachers' Estimates of Percent of
Students with Preschool Experience

Grade	Estimated Percent		Number of Teachers Reporting
	m	s.d.	
2	24	29	547
4	19	25	497
6	15	24	340

that the upper grade teachers were simply less familiar with the students' backgrounds and were inclined toward conservative estimates.

Potential for School Success

To what extent do teachers expect future academic success from students who have received compensatory reading services in the elementary school? Do children profit from the supportive instruction they receive? Are they expected to succeed in future academic endeavors, or will they find academic pursuits difficult and unfulfilling? Teachers were asked to state their opinions about these questions. In response to a question asking how far they expected the average student in their classes to progress in school *if given the opportunity,* about 85 percent of the teachers indicated that the students might graduate from high school, and almost a third believed the students capable of college level work. However, teachers were less optimistic about what would actually happen. Nearly 25 percent indicated that many students would become high school dropouts, and only 15 percent judged that the typical student would actually reach college. In short, they believed that, although students in compensatory reading programs were behind in the development of reading skills, they were intellectually capable and motivated to succeed in school, if given a chance.

Physical and Psychological Problems

Many educators have sought to identify physical and psychological factors associated with school failure. The literature on reading failure is filled with discussions about causal factors ranging from vision and hearing deficiencies to disorders of perceptual integration and minimal brain dysfunction. Teachers were asked to estimate the percent of pupils in their classes who were experiencing one or more difficulties linked to low achievement in reading. Table 3-4 summarizes these data by grade level.

On the whole, the teachers thought that the incidence of physical problems among children enrolled in compensatory reading classes was low and not significantly different from the proportion of such problems in the general population of elementary school children. For emotional and home related factors, the percentage is considerably greater. There is no detail on the nature of the emotional problems reported, but we suspect these showed up as behavioral and discipline problems at school. These may relate solely to school failure, but the fact that the proportion is relatively constant across grade levels suggests that problems of personal adjustment, troubled family interactions, and other "outside" factors were interfering with school achievement. These problems were more common in ungraded compensatory reading classes, supporting the suspicion that such classes were probably composed of children with serious learning difficulties.

Absenteeism

Success in any program depends, at least in part, upon regular attendance in that program. In turn, regular attendance is partly related to physical and psychological well-being. Teachers were asked to estimate the rate and causes of absenteeism. On the average, absenteeism was low in compensatory classes—about three percent, with a range from zero to ten percent. This suggests that attendance in compensatory classes was about as stable as in regular classrooms.

The causes of absenteeism as estimated by the teachers are reported in Table 3-5. As in regular classrooms, children were most often absent from compensatory reading classes because of illness. However, teachers, especially those at the upper level, frequently attributed absenteeism to family-related problems. Whether these same trends would be found in regular classrooms cannot be reliably determined from the data.

Family Background

A descriptive profile of "poor readers" in compensatory programs requires that we consider social and economic characteristics of the students' families. Historically, the notion of compensatory education grew out of a concern for economically and experientially deprived children, and for those from language and cultural backgrounds different from the typical classroom teacher. Several surveys have established significantly higher percentages of reading retardation and school dropout

Table 3-4

Estimated Percentage of Students
with Specific Problems Linked with Reading Failure

| Problems | GRADE | | | |
	2nd (n=582 to 635)	4th (n=565 to 596)	6th (n=411 to 429)	Ungraded (n=75 to 83)
Speech	10 (14)	6 (10)	7 (13)	10 (12)
Vision	6 (10)	8 (12)	9 (13)	8 (12)
Hearing	3 (7)	3 (6)	3 (6)	5 (9)
Frequent Illness	7 (11)	7 (11)	8 (13)	6 (8)
Mental Retardation	2 (6)	3 (7)	4 (11)	8 (17)
Emotional Problems	15 (19)	16 (19)	17 (20)	21 (23)
Unstable Families	21 (22)	20 (21)	22 (23)	27 (24)

Table 3-5
Percentage of Teachers Citing Causes of Absenteeism
in Compensatory Reading Classes, by Grade Level

Causes	GRADE			
	2nd (n =664)	4th (n =630)	6th (n =456)	Ungraded (n =83)
Pupil Illness	93	93	91	93
Family Illness	19	22	24	28
Lack of Parental Concern	40	41	42	42
Needed at Home	17	28	39	34
Suspension/ Expulsion	2	3	6	8
Other	7	6	7	8

among minority group members and the poor (Mayeske & Beaton, 1975; Coleman, 1966). The principal survey provided school-wide estimates of family composition (Chapter 2). However we also have the estimates from teachers of compensatory reading classes about the makeup of their particular classes.

Racial and National Origin

Table 3-6 shows the breakdown by grade of the major racial and national groups attending compensatory reading classes at the time of this survey, as estimated by the teachers.

It is a mistaken picture of compensatory reading programs that portrays them as largely populated by minority students. Caucasians (i.e., "other whites") made up the majority of the students in more than two-thirds of these classes. Black or Spanish surname children comprised the majority in less than one in five classrooms. Children from Oriental, American Indian, and "Other" backgrounds were overall a small proportion of the compensatory reading program enrollments. These data agree well with the national sample from the NIE study of compensatory programs (NIE, 1976), which found that 69 percent of the students in compensatory classrooms were Caucasian, 24 percent Black, 6 percent Spanish, and 1 percent other. However, the NIE survey also showed that a greater representation of minorities among the students in the classroom specifically identified for compensatory assistance. The percentages were 54

Table 3-6

Teacher Estimates of Percentage of Racial and National Groups in Compensatory Reading Programs.
Percentage of Teachers in Each Estimation Category by Grade Level

Teacher Estimate of Percentage Families in Each Category	2nd (n=664)						4th (n=630)						6th (n=456)						Ungraded (n=83)					
	C	B	S	O	A	N	C	B	S	O	A	N	C	B	S	O	A	N	C	B	S	O	A	N
75 - 100	60	9	1	0	0	0	60	9	5	0	0	0	57	10	1	0	0	0	54	16	1	0	0	0
50 - 75	12	5	1	0	0	0	12	5	3	0	0	0	12	5	2	0	0	0	15	4	3	0	0	0
25 - 50	11	9	2	1	0	1	9	9	4	0	1	0	12	10	5	0	0	0	6	11	1	0	0	0
1 - 25	8	16	13	2	2	2	9	15	11	2	5	2	10	11	12	3	3	2	11	24	13	7	12	1
0	7	40	54	67	68	31	5	38	55	67	64	28	7	39	48	61	61	25	10	36	71	80	75	35
No response	5	22	28	30	30	66	5	23	27	31	31	70	7	24	32	36	36	73	1	8	11	13	12	64
Average Percentage	72	21	6	1	1	1	72	21	7	1	1	1	71	23	8	1	1	1	67	27	5	1	1	1

GRADE — GROUP[a]

Note a - C = Caucasian, B = Black, S = Spanish Surname, O = Oriental, A = Native American, N = Other

percent Caucasian, 35 percent Black, 10 percent Spanish surname, and 1 percent other.

Comparison of racial and national representation in compensatory reading classes with that reported by principals for the school as a whole (Table 2-4) shows no major disagreements. There are few grade level trends, except that upper grade teachers were more likely to give no response.

Language

About 25 percent of the teachers at all grades reported that a noticeable proportion of their students came from homes in which English was not the dominant language. Table 3-7 shows some details on the distribution of non-English speaking families in this survey. Spanish-base languages dominate. These results suggest that differing language backgrounds could be a significant obstacle to reading achievement for a significant number of students in elementary schools (Engle, 1975; Gonzalez, 1977) and point up the importance of bilingual programs. More than one in twenty teachers reported that at least half the class came from a family in which the dominant language was not English. Incidentally, the 1970 Census notes that approximately 21 percent of the national population spoke a language other than English as a first language (U.S. Department of Commerce, 1970).

Parent Occupations

The proportion of children from various economic backgrounds can also be inferred from the teacher estimates of parent occupations (Table 3-8). At all grades, the teachers estimated that skilled and unskilled occupations were most common for their students' parents. Unemployment was estimated at about 10 percent. Roughly one in seven families was white collar, and about one in ten was either business or professional.

· A comparison of these percentages with the principals' estimates of the distribution of parental occupations in the total school populations (Table 2-2) shows the teachers' estimates to be more strongly weighted toward the lower-income occupations. For instance, principals estimated that about half of the families in the entire school were white collar, business or professional; the teachers' estimates for the same categories added up to about a quarter of the families, while the differences between the principals' estimates for the total school and teachers' estimates for their compensatory classes were rather striking; the meaning of these differences is not altogether clear. It may be that families of compensatory students are from different occupational strata than the families of the school as a whole; it may be that the principals and teachers simply differ in their judgments. The U.S. Census report of 1970 lends support to the inference that families of compensatory students are from different

Table 3-7
Percentage of Teachers Reporting Significant Number
of Students from Non-English Language Homes

Language	GRADE			
	2nd (n=664)	4th (n=630)	6th (n=456)	Ungraded (n=83)
American Indian	1	2	1	1
Chinese	1	1	2	1
Japanese	1	1	2	0
Spanish/Portuguese	17	17	21	19
French	3	2	2	4
Other	7	6	9	7

occupational strata. About 25 percent of the employed population was described as white collar, 10 percent business/management, and 14 percent professional, while about 28 percent were skilled workers and about 20 percent were unskilled and service workers. The principals' estimates substantially agree with the census report. The school population reflects the national income distribution. The students in compensatory classes, according to their teachers, were more likely to come from lower income families.

Summary and Conclusions

The ETS survey showed that students were selected for compensatory reading programs primarily on the basis of low reading test scores and teacher recommendation. Membership in a target group and family referral were secondary considerations. Children from disadvantaged backgrounds made up a quarter to a third of the enrollment in compensatory classes. About three out of five students in these classes were boys. Many had been in compensatory programs previously, and there is some evidence of retention in the early grades or of late entrance to school.

These children were diverse in cultural and ethnic background, in socioeconomic level, and in family occupation. Lower-income and minority families were more common in compensatory classes than in the general population, as might be expected. There was also evidence of substantial segregation across the sample of schools.

Teachers expressed several opinions about the causes of poor reading achievement in the compensatory classes. On the whole, they reported a

Table 3-8

Teacher Estimates of Percentage of Parents in Occupational Categories
Percentage of Teachers in Each Estimation Category by Grade Level

Teacher Estimate of Percentage Families in Each Category	GRADE																							
	2nd (n=664)						4th (n=630)						6th (n=456)						Ungraded (n=83)					
	GROUP a																							
	P	B	W	S	U	N	P	B	W	S	U	N	P	B	W	S	U	N	P	B	W	S	U	N
90 – 100	0	0	1	2	6	1	0	0	1	2	6	1	0	0	1	4	5	0	0	0	0	1	5	0
50 – 90	0	2	3	6	19	4	0	0	5	7	17	2	0	0	4	5	19	2	0	0	4	6	20	5
10 – 50	5	9	23	29	33	10	5	8	25	29	32	10	3	10	24	30	29	12	0	4	26	32	33	10
0 – 10	21	29	39	32	27	38	26	38	38	34	25	39	26	38	41	36	29	39	26	42	43	37	28	53
0	63	49	25	21	9	33	56	42	21	18	9	32	57	38	19	14	8	29	62	42	16	12	6	19
No response	10	11	11	8	7	17	12	13	10	12	10	17	14	13	12	11	9	18	12	11	12	12	7	13
Average Percentage	4	6	13	19	32	10	4	6	15	19	32	8	3	6	15	20	31	8	2	5	14	21	33	10

Note a - P = Professional, B = Business and Managerial, W = White Collar, S = Skilled and Farm owners

U = Unskilled and Service, N = Not Employed

low incidence of physical problems, probably not significantly different from the population at large. Psychological and sociological problems associated with home background were more frequently cited at all grade levels. Absenteeism was also attributed to home-related difficulties.

Teachers of compensatory classes were generally optimistic about their students' potential for future academic success. They were less sanguine about what would actually happen to the students, and many teachers expressed a concern that many of their students might be high school dropouts. There are many reasons why the student might fail to complete a basic secondary education. One of the more hopeful aspects of the survey was the teachers' judgments that these low achieving students were intellectually capable and that with proper instruction and adequate motivation they could become proficient readers and perform successfully in school.

Chapter 4
Teacher Characteristics

Jerome C. Harste
Darryl J. Strickler
Indiana University

The purpose of this chapter is to describe and illustrate the professional characteristics of the sample of 1750 second-, fourth-, and sixth-grade teachers in the Educational Testing Service (ETS) Phase I study of compensatory reading programs. The teachers of ungraded classes were not included in this analysis. Professional preparation, teaching experience, job satisfaction, attitude toward students and school administrators, and the teacher's perception of the effectiveness of compensatory reading programs will be discussed in the first part of the chapter. The latter section of the chapter addresses teacher beliefs as they relate to the teaching of reading generally, and more particularly to the teaching of reading to disadvantaged children.

Before immersing ourselves in the details of the data, it may help to present an overview of our findings. The following profile of the "typical" teacher of compensatory reading can be reconstructed from the data on teacher characteristics in the survey:

> The teacher is a white female with three or more years of teaching experience, and holds a regular certificate with post-certification training in the diagnosis and treatment of reading programs. She believes, among other things, that a) methods are more important than materials in the teaching of reading, b) the teacher's ability is more important than either method or material in the teaching of reading, and c) a wrong response can be as useful as a correct response in teaching reading.

With this overview of the "typical" teacher of compensatory reading in mind, let us move to a consideration of the data base from which the profile was constructed.

Demographic Data

Teacher-Pupil Ethnic Match

Teachers were asked to indicate if most of their students were of the same racial or national origin as they were, and the percentage of pupils in their compensatory reading classes who were members of various racial and national origins. A cross analysis of the data suggested that in areas where there was a concentration of minority pupils, there was also a concentration of minority group reading teachers. While this correspondence is not perfect, 80 times out of 100 the trend prevails.

Given a high concentration of pupils of one racial or national origin (76 to 100 percent), the probability of finding a white teacher in the classroom, if the students were also white, was 95 times out of 100. For blacks, given the same concentration, the probability of finding a black teacher was 48 times out of 100. For Spanish surnamed children, the probability was 17 times out of 100. For American Indian, Oriental, and children of other racial or national origins, the probability of finding a high concentration of these minority pupils in one area was so low that no meaningful statistics could be determined.

Taking into account the distribution of students, we were able to estimate that about 85 percent of the teachers were Caucasian, about 11 percent Black, 1 percent Spanish surnamed, and the remainder divided among Asian-American, Native-American, and other. These percentages agree almost exactly with the report of the Equal Employment Opportunity Commission (1975). A more recent survey (NIE, 1976) found that 77 percent of compensatory education teachers were Caucasian, 20 percent Black, and 2 percent Spanish surnamed, revealing a more substantial representation of minority teachers.

Sex

The large majority of the teachers in the ETS survey (88 percent) was female. Only one percent of the second-grade teachers in the sample were male; by fourth and sixth grades, the number of males increased to eight and 34 percent, respectively. Women predominated as teachers of elementary school children, but the higher the grade level, the more likely the teacher was to be a male. However, even in the upper elementary school grades, the probability of a female teacher was almost twice as great as the probability of a male teacher.

Preparation and Experience

Academic Preparation

Elementary teachers of compensatory reading typically prepared for their professional responsibilities by earning a bachelor's degree (97 percent) and, in many cases, they also held a master's degree (24 percent). All of these findings show that compensatory teachers in 1971 differed little from teachers nationwide (NEA, 1972). Grade level trends are observable in Table 4-1. First, the percentage of teachers with no degree or an associate of arts was slight and about the same at all grade levels. Second, and more noticeable, the percentage of teachers who held a master's degree increased consistently with grade level.

The data in Table 4-2 do not say anything about the quantity and quality of coursework in the reading programs completed by the teachers. The survey did include a question related to special training in the diagnosis and treatment of reading difficulties. In response to the question "Have you had any special training in the diagnosis and treatment of reading difficulties?" 57 percent of the teachers confirmed that they had received this specialized training at the graduate level, about 28 percent at the undergraduate level, and about 16 percent through inservice activities or through on-the-job training. Grade-level trends in special training are shown in Table 4-2.

These figures are more meaningful in the context of other data on training in reading typically provided at the baccalaureate level. Roeder, Beal, and Eller (1973) found that 80 percent of the four-year colleges and universities in their survey required only one course in the teaching of reading for pre-service teachers. Of these, 17 percent combined reading with another methods course. Approximately 3 percent of the colleges and universities surveyed reported that they required additional courses in reading beyond the basic course. Given this information we can con-

Table 4-1
Highest College Degree Earned

	Grade		
Highest Degree Earned	2nd (n=664)	4th (n=630)	6th (n=455)
None	2%	1%	1%
Associate of Arts	1%	1%	2%
Bachelor of Arts	77%	72%	68%
Master of Arts	20%	25%	29%

Harste and Strickler

Table 4-2

Percentage of Teachers with Special Training in Diagnosis and
Treatment of Reading Problems, as a Function of Grade Level

	Grade		
	2nd (n =659)	4th (n =627)	6th (n =455)
Have Received Training	60	57	55
Level of Training[a]	(N=288)	(N=264)	(N=197)
Undergraduate	26	30	27
Graduate	55	53	52
Inservice	15	13	15
On-the-Job & Other	4	4	5

Note a. Number answering question 6a on level of special

training

clude that almost half of the teachers in the ETS survey may have had
only a single general course in reading.

What training should the elementary teacher have in order to be
adequately prepared to carry out reading instruction? The Professional
Standards and Ethics Committee of the International Reading Association
recommends the following minimum standards of academic training for
elementary school teachers (IRA, undated).

A minimum of six semester hours, or the equivalent, in an accred-
ited reading course or courses.

One or more courses for elementary teachers covering each of the
following areas:

General Background
   The nature of language
   Psychology of the reading process

Interrelationship of activities and outcomes in the four language arts

Nature and scope of the reading program

Reading Skills and Abilities

Prereading readiness abilities

Readiness for reading at any level

Word recognition skills (including word analysis)

Vocabulary development

Reading comprehension abilities, including critical reading

Interpretive oral reading

Diagnosis and Remedial Teaching

Techniques for evaluation of progress

Difficulties frequently experienced by children in learning to read

Diagnostic techniques that can be used by the classroom teacher

Differentiation of instruction to fit individual capabilities

Corrective methods for use in the classroom

Organization of the Reading Program

Classroom organization for reading

Varied approaches to reading instruction

Planning a reading lesson

Materials

Knowledge and use of basic and supplementary materials of instruction

Selection of suitable reading materials

Knowledge of children's literature

Application of Reading Skills

Skills needed for reading in content fields

Qualities to be appreciated in literature

Fostering lifetime use of reading

By these standards, it appears that as many as three out of every four teachers of compensatory reading probably had not met IRA's recommended standards for training.

In a follow-up study on teacher training, Morrison and Austin (1977) reported significant steps by colleges and universities to meet the recommendations made in *The Torch Lighters* (Austin, Morrison, & Kenney, 1961), which was a landmark study on the status of teacher training programs. While progress was evident in the 1977 survey, their conclusion stated again the importance of teacher training as a priority concern:

> Throughout this report, and the earlier one, the teacher is viewed as the leader of the movement to improve the teaching of reading in the nation's schools. This is not to say that the teacher alone is responsible for student success. New

teaching methodologies, new materials, and new organizational plans will continue to be promoted in the future. Unless the teacher can select wisely and adapt ideas for use with individual children in different settings, little progress can be expected. (p. 77)

Teaching certification. About 85 percent of teachers of compensatory reading in the ETS study held regular (i.e., permanent) teaching credentials. Roughly 15 percent held temporary (or provisional) certificates, and a little less than one percent lacked a teaching certificate altogether. Second-grade teachers were only a little more likely to have temporary certificates (16 percent) than fourth- and sixth-grade teachers (14 and 13 percent respectively).

Teaching Experience

Most of the teachers in the survey had been in the profession for some time; the median was about ten years, which agrees closely with the NEA survey (NEA, 1972). More than 80 percent of the teachers of compensatory reading in the ETS study had three or more years of teaching experience. The trends in teaching experience are similar for teachers over grade levels (Table 4-3). About a quarter of the teachers at each grade level had taught between 10 and 20 years. Another one in five had taught for more than 20 years. Less than one teacher in ten had taught one year or less.

In Table 4-4 are the data on the number of years teachers of compensatory reading had taught in their present school assignment. Here again, the trends are similar across all three grade levels. About two-thirds of the teachers had taught six or less years in the school in which they were teaching at the time of the study.

These data indicate a moderate level of turnover. About 60 percent of the teachers had taught in their present school for more than three years. The relative stability may be a positive sign. To be sure, teacher turnover may have been high in some schools; this would not reflect in the aggregate data in Table 4-4.

Teacher Satisfaction

Teachers in the ETS study were asked to rate their satisfaction with: a) the ability of the student body in their school, b) the attitudes of the student body, c) other teachers in their school, d) their school's administration, e) the overall philosophy of education in their school, and f) the physical facilities of their school. The data on these ratings are shown in Table 4-5.

The most positive ratings were given to the school's faculty (other teachers) and the overall philosophy of education, and there was least satisfaction with the attitudes and ability of students. Again the data show

Table 4-3
Years of Teaching Experience as a Function of Grade Level
Percent of Teachers in Each Category

Years of Teaching Experience	Grade		
	2nd (n=664)	4th (n=630)	6th (n=455)
1 year or less	9	6	9
More than 1 year, less than 3 years	11	11	13
At least 3 years, less than 6 years	18	18	18
At least 6 years, less than 10 years	14	18	20
At least 10 years, less than 20 years	29	27	24
20 years or more	20	21	17

little difference across grade levels, except for physical facilities, which left the upper grade teachers less happy.

The data presented in Table 4-5 might easily lead to the conclusion that teachers of compensatory reading are, for the most part, satisfied with the working environment in which they find themselves. However, the fact that teachers were least positive about their students' abilities and attitudes is of some concern because of possible influence of teacher expectations on pupil learning. If teachers of compensatory reading were dissatisfied with the abilities or attitudes of their students, they might not expect their students to achieve, an expectation which might in turn influence how they teach the students.

Teachers were asked two other questions which relate to satisfaction with the program:

Harste and Strickler

Do you believe that compensatory programs are generally worthwhile?

Do you believe that there is a sound basis in educational policy for giving compensatory programs to disadvantaged students at extra per pupil cost [are compensatory programs worth the extra cost]?

The teachers' responses to these two questions, shown in Table 4-6, reveal a general trend to believe that the programs are valuable. The teachers were a bit skeptical about whether the benefits justified the additional cost. Nonetheless, the data clearly reflect the fact that the majority of teachers in compensatory programs believed that what they were doing was worthwhile and was worth the additional expense.

Table 4-4

Years of Teaching Experience in Present Assignment
as a Function of Grade Level
Percent of Teachers in Each Category

Years in Present Assignment	Grade		
	2nd (n=664)	4th (n=630)	6th (n=456)
1 year or less	19	18	25
More than 1 year, less than 3 years	19	22	19
At least 3 years, less than 6 years	24	27	24
At least 6 years, less than 10 years	16	16	15
At least 10 years, less than 20 years	18	14	14
20 years or more	4	4	2

Table 4-5
Distribution of Teacher Satisfaction Ratings
Percentage of Teachers Marking Each Rating Category

Satisfaction with:	Second (N=658 to 662)				Fourth (N=621 to 627)				Sixth (N=451 to 455)			
	Highly Positive	Moderately Positive	Moderately Negative	Highly Negative	Highly Positive	Moderately Positive	Moderately Negative	Highly Negative	Highly Positive	Moderately Positive	Moderately Negative	Highly Negative
Ability of Student Body	24	59	14	3	21	63	13	4	17	60	20	3
Attitudes of Student Body	21	53	21	5	18	53	24	6	14	50	30	6
Faculty (teachers)	57	39	4	1	55	40	4	1	54	40	5	2
Administration	49	38	10	3	47	41	10	2	46	40	11	4
Overall Philosophy of education	40	51	7	2	40	50	8	2	29	55	12	3
Physical Facilities (buildings, etc.)	32	50	14	3	36	45	15	4	28	51	15	6

Note: Sample size varies slightly due to nonresponse rate

Harste and Strickler

Table 4-6
Teacher Judgments of Program Value
Percentage of Teachers Responding on Each Category

Questions	GRADE														
	Second (N=659)					Fourth (N=629)					Sixth (N=456)				
	Definite Yes	Probable Yes	Undecided	Probable No	Definite No	Definite Yes	Probable Yes	Undecided	Probable No	Definite No	Definite Yes	Probable Yes	Undecided	Probable No	Definite No
Are compensatory programs worthwhile?	56	35	7	1	1	59	34	7	1	0	53	36	8	2	0
Are compensatory programs worth the extra cost?	49	32	14	3	2	49	33	14	3	1	47	34	12	4	3

Teacher Attitudes about Reading

Teachers were presented with sixteen propositions related to the academic capabilities of disadvantaged pupils and were asked to indicate the degree to which they agreed or disagreed with each statement. For purposes of presentation, the statements have been arranged in two categories: statements which deal with the teaching of reading in general, and statements which deal more specifically with the teaching of reading to disadvantaged children.

General Attitudes toward the Teaching of Reading

Table 4-7 presents several statements which deal generally with teaching of reading. The data show that teachers strongly endorsed the notion that the teacher's ability is the important variable in the teaching of reading. Next most important were methods, followed by materials. There were no significant differential trends over grades. Interestingly, this ranking—teachers, methods, materials—seems inversely related to how most school systems spend monies on the reading program. Our experience suggests that most districts invest the largest amount in materials and the least amount in teacher inservice training. The teachers' ranking of these program components parallels the conclusions reached by several researchers. For example, one of the best known research efforts related to the teaching of reading is the Cooperative Research Program in First Grade Reading Instruction (Bond & Dykstra, 1967). The cooperative program attempted to discover whether any approaches to initial reading instruction would produce superior reading and spelling achievement in the early elementary grades. Various instructional approaches, including the linguistic, basal, language experience, and i.t.a., were evaluated using standardized measures of reading achievement. Despite problems in making sure that each approach was used in a "pure" form, the study's findings and conclusions were clearcut. Children learned to read about equally well by a variety of materials and methods; ". . . no one approach is so distinctively better in all situations and respects than the others that it should be considered the one best method and the one to be used exclusively" (Bond and Dykstra, 1967). Improved reading achievement did not depend primarily on the approach or method. The authors continue:

> Future research might well center on teaching and learning situation characteristics. . . . The tremendous range among classrooms within any method points out the importance of elements in the learning situation over and above the methods employed. *To improve reading it is necessary to train better teachers of reading rather than to expect a panacea in the form of materials.* (p. 11)

Harris and Morrison (1969) reiterate this conclusion. These authors reported a three-year study of two approaches to teaching reading: basal readers versus language experience. They found, as did Bond and Dykstra,

Table 4-7

General Attitudes toward the Teaching of Reading
Percentage of Teachers Marking each Category

| | GRADE | | | | | | | | | | | | | | |
| | Second (N=664) | | | | | Fourth (N=630) | | | | | Sixth (N=456) | | | | |
Statement	Definite Yes	Probable Yes	Undecided	Probable No	Definite No	Definite Yes	Probable Yes	Undecided	Probable No	Definite No	Definite Yes	Probable Yes	Undecided	Probable No	Definite No
Materials are more important than methods in the teaching of reading	5	5	9	62	24	5	5	11	62	21	2	6	10	59	23
Methods are more important than materials in the teaching of reading	17	52	11	17	2	15	52	13	18	1	15	54	11	18	2
The teacher's ability is more important than either methods or materials in the teaching of reading	32	48	10	9	1	26	52	12	9	1	28	47	15	8	1

that differences in reading scores *within* each method were much larger than differences between methods and approaches:

> The results of the study have indicated that the teacher is far more important than the method. Clearly procedures such as smaller classes and provision of auxiliary personnel may continue to give disappointing results if teaching skills are not improved. It is recommended, therefore, that in-service workshops and expert consultive help be provided for all teachers and especially for those with minimal experience. (p. 339)

Studies such as these have helped to establish the importance of the teacher variable in the teaching of reading. In light of the rather widespread acceptance of the importance of the teacher variable in reading, one might well wonder why we haven't explored the variable more thoroughly. Currently there are a handful of researchers who have explored and who are continuing to explore this area (Barr, 1974-75; Bussis, Chittenden, & Amarel, 1976; Duffy, 1977; Harste & Burke, in press; McDonald & Elias, 1976; Stallings & Kaskowitz, 1974). Until we know more about specific factors related to the teacher variable and the relationships of these factors to instructional decisions and classroom behaviors, our knowledge of the importance of the teacher variable is likely to be of interest but not of particular help by itself.

Specific Attitudes about the Teaching of Reading to Disadvantaged Children

Table 4-8 presents the teachers' judgments about several statements concerning the teaching of reading to disadvantaged children. We should note that underlying these statements are some unflattering assumptions about what teachers thought of children who were enrolled in compensatory reading programs. The wording of the statements constrained the teachers' responses. For this reason, the results reflect in part the opinions of the researchers and consultants who assisted in the process of instrument development. On the other hand, teachers had the option of agreeing or disagreeing with each statement, or giving no answer—the nonresponse rate was less than one percent.

The following is a summary of what appear to be the dominant beliefs held by the teachers in this survey:

1. Disadvantaged pupils want to learn, but they do not have the proper background for school work (*c, d,* and *l*).
2. Disadvantaged children have different linguistic experiences than advantaged children (*k*).
3. Learning to verbalize complete thoughts is particularly important for disadvantaged children (*m*).
4. Improving the student's self-image as a learner is particularly important for disadvantaged children (*n*).

Viewed from the bright side, these ratings suggest that today's teacher of reading is aware of not only the linguistic and cognitive nature of the

Harste and Strickler

Table 4-8

Specific Attitudes toward the Teaching of Reading to Disadvantaged Students
Percentage of Teachers Marking each Category

Statement	GRADE														
	Second (N=664)					Fourth (N=630)					Sixth (N=456)				
	Definite Yes	Probable Yes	Undecided	Probable No	Definite No	Definite Yes	Probable Yes	Undecided	Probable No	Definite No	Definite Yes	Probable Yes	Undecided	Probable No	Definite No
a. With proper instruction disadvantaged students can learn about as well as any other pupils	9	50	18	20	3	12	46	18	22	1	11	47	17	22	3
b. No matter how good the instruction these pupils, they will always score lower than middle class children	1	16	22	47	14	1	17	21	48	13	1	17	16	51	13
c. These children do not want to learn	1	2	7	55	34	1	2	10	51	36	1	4	6	52	36
d. These pupils want to learn but they do not have the right background for school work	12	64	13	9	2	14	54	18	12	2	13	62	12	11	2

Table 4-8 (continued)

Statement	Second (N=664)					Fourth (N=630)					Sixth (N=456)				
	Definite Yes	Probable Yes	Undecided	Probable No	Definite No	Definite Yes	Probable Yes	Undecided	Probable No	Definite No	Definite Yes	Probable Yes	Undecided	Probable No	Definite No
e. It has been sufficiently proven that such pupils will never do as well as other students	1	6	27	49	18	1	6	23	50	21	1	6	24	49	20
f. These children have more trouble learning to read than advantaged children	15	64	11	9	2	14	64	13	8	1	13	64	11	10	1
j. These children have a shorter attention span than advantaged	9	49	23	16	2	9	45	21	21	3	8	47	24	19	2
k. These children have different linguistic experiences than advantaged	21	66	9	3	1	20	69	7	3	1	18	69	9	4	1
i. These children are disadvantaged mainly in that they do not have same foundation of concepts as advantaged	17	62	12	8	0	12	59	17	10	1	11	60	19	9	1

Harste and Strickler

Table 4-8 (continued)

Statement	Second (N=664)					Fourth (N=630)					Sixth (N=456)				
	Definite Yes	Probable Yes	Undecided	Probable No	Definite No	Definite Yes	Probable Yes	Undecided	Probable No	Definite No	Definite Yes	Probable Yes	Undecided	Probable No	Definite No
m. Learning to verbalize complete thoughts is particularly important for disadvantaged children	16	67	11	4	0	14	70	11	4	1	15	64	15	5	0
n. Improving the student's self-image as a learner is particularly important for these children	11	51	21	15	1	13	48	23	13	2	13	47	24	15	1
o. The ability to ask questions which require a complete answer is extremely important in teaching reading to these children	11	51	21	15	1	13	48	23	13	2	13	47	24	15	1
q. These children often have lower aspirations than the advantaged	10	53	18	16	2	8	54	18	16	4	10	55	15	16	3

GRADE

reading process but the affective dimension as well. Collectively, teacher response patterns stated a basic and clear-cut belief about reading: language, thought, and how one feels about oneself are all important dimensions of the teaching of reading. Those of us who agree on the importance of these elements can be pleased with the teachers' awareness.

On the other side, one may feel sorry for the "disadvantaged child." Clearly, teachers did not attribute much to him beyond desire: He lacks the foundation of concepts of his advantaged peers. He can't verbalize complete thoughts. He has a poor self-image.

What underlying beliefs might have lead teachers to agree with such statements? Teacher responses are founded upon experience. Many of these teachers must have learned from their own classroom experience that disadvantaged children have more trouble learning to read than do advantaged children. There must have been some reason why they attributed this difficulty to the belief that the children had language and cognitive deficiencies.

Standing counter to these beliefs is the body of language research which concludes that the language of the "disadvantaged" is not deficient, but different (Labov, 1969; Halliday, 1970). According to this position, the disadvantaged child's language is a system, as whole and as functional as that which the teacher speaks. The "disadvantaged" child does not have an incomplete system; he has different semantic and conceptual knowledge, springing from different background experiences, and there is research evidence that what we get from an experience is determined by what we started with conceptually in the first place (Anderson, Spiro, & Montague, 1977).

The teachers' conclusion that the language and thought of disadvantaged students were deficient might well have been based on comparison with relatively more advanced students. Since sociologists and psychologists maintain that the language of the two groups is comparable in function—disadvantaged students do communicate and do use language to solve problems (Halliday, 1970; Cook-Gumperz & Corsaro, 1977)—teachers might have based their judgments of deficiency on the surface features of disadvantaged children's speech and thought. The particular words chosen by a child, his phrasing and dialect, his grammar, his lack of interest in solving problems that seem unfamiliar or irrelevant—all of these aspects of the disadvantaged student's behavior are different from what the teacher may expect from a model student. However, to attach great importance to deviations in the surface structure of language may be unfortunate, especially for reading. For example, Goodman (1965) has shown that children can alter the surface structure of the text and still reconstruct the author's meaning. Reading is a receptive language process, and the criteria of language production go beyond what is needed to read. In fact, when children make surface level alterations to the text in the direction of their preferred language ("be going" for "is going") and cognitive forms ("rough and tough" for "huff and puff"), this is evidence that the child has understood.

The present survey provides only a modest glimpse of what teachers think about the disadvantaged students in their compensatory reading classes. The teachers' beliefs about student shortcomings in language and thought may reflect their view of reading as a translation process requiring precise reproduction. Such beliefs may spring from a lack of information about alternate dialects and language forms and an attitude that only conventional forms are acceptable. Whatever the case, upwards of 70 percent of the teachers in the survey agreed with the statements. To the extent that these responses lead to instruction in which disadvantaged students are not adequately served, we face an inservice training task of considerable magnitude and urgency.

Summary

The ETS survey yielded a profile of the "typical" compensatory reading teacher in 1972 as white, female, with about five to ten years of experience, and certificated and specially trained in reading problems. The teacher tended to be satisfied with her colleagues, less satisfied with the students, convinced that compensatory programs made a difference, but skeptical about whether the benefits justified the costs. She thought that the effectiveness of compensatory reading instruction depended most on the teacher, then on the method, and least on the materials. She also believed that the reading problems of disadvantaged children reflected, at least in part, deficiencies in the children's thought and language. This belief may interfere with the teacher's appreciation of the poverty child's language and may lead the teacher to expect less of the child than he is actually capable of achieving.

Chapter 5

Organization For Instruction

John J. Pikulski
Irwin S. Kirsch
University of Delaware

The relationships among students and teachers, the division of students into classes and instructional groups, and the scheduling of learning activities during the school day—all of these decisions are involved in what we mean by organization for instruction. This chapter will summarize data on organization for compensatory reading instruction from the Educational Testing Service (ETS) survey. We examine organization for instruction at different grade levels and make some effort to determine the effects of global variables (e.g., geographic region) on organizational variables (e.g., amount of time per instructional period).

This chapter consists of four sections. The first looks at overall school organization, including the grade level structure and the relations among school personnel in the reading program. The second section examines characteristics of classes in the school, including class size and the number of pupils. In the third section we consider the features of instructional groups within classes, such as the size of reading groups, the criteria for grouping, and the frequency with which groups are changed. The final section deals with scheduling, the length and number of instructional periods, and the scheduling of compensatory classes.

School Organization

Graded versus Ungraded Classes

Principals indicated whether their schools were graded, ungraded, or some combination of the two. Graded classes were by far the most common form of organization within a school. Eighty-two percent of the principals reported graded classes for kindergarten through eighth grade; nine percent reported having classes which were ungraded, and nine percent reported a combination of graded and ungraded classes.

The widespread reliance on grading is not necessarily a desirable state of affairs. There is some evidence that student performance is superior when an ungraded organizational system is used (Machiele, 1965; Brody, 1970). However, other studies (Jones, Moore, & VanDevender, 1967; Hopkins, Oldridge, & Williamson, 1965) have found no significant differences between the reading achievement of students in graded and ungraded programs. In interpreting these null results we are mindful of the comment by Austin and Morrison (1963) that *"While there are certain advantages to utilization of non-graded plans,* the staff found that instruction offered in non-graded schools varied little from that offered in graded ones" (p. 86, emphasis added).

About a third of the administrators in the Austin and Morrison survey favored a nongraded plan for the school. However, ". . . despite the fact that they favored the nongraded plan, these respondents doubted if such an organizational plan would become a reality in their school systems. They cited parental and teacher resistance . . . as well as the lack of expertise on the part of colleagues who would be responsible for initiating or organizing any revolutionary program as the primary deterrents" (p. 82). There were fears that an ungraded plan would be difficult to administer, would revert to a graded structure, and would reveal that teachers have been poorly prepared by their preservice programs for working in such a plan. These reasons for avoiding an ungraded plan are probably among the ones that would be given today.

Support Personnel

Teachers were asked about the professionals, paraprofessionals, and volunteers available to them in the school. Table 5-1 shows their responses. Reading specialists, remedial reading teachers, and supervisors were the most frequently cited support personnel groups. Over a third of the teachers reported that reading specialists were "frequently" available, but an equal number of teachers reported that specialists are "rarely" or "never" available. It is hard to conceive of a well-planned, carefully administered compensatory reading program that would not include such support.

Paraprofessionals and aides were reported as "frequently available" by less than a third of the respondents. The data suggest that volunteers and tutors are infrequent. The NIE (1976b) survey of compensatory education found that the regular classroom teacher provided compensatory reading instruction to 53 percent of the identified students, whereas specialists had some contact with 75 percent of the students, and teacher

Table 5-1
Teachers' Estimates of Available Support Personnel

	Percent Responding				
	Frequent	Occasional	Rare	Not Available	Number
Remedial reading teacher or supervisor	37	25	13	25	1606
Resource teacher	19	19	14	48	1433
Other professionals (counselors, psychologists, etc.)	11	34	31	23	1511
Paraprofessionals or aides	30	17	11	42	1541
Parent or other volunteer	7	13	17	63	1435
Student teacher	5	15	8	72	1422
Media specialist	8	13	15	63	1389
Older student	7	16	16	61	1422

aides with 50 percent. The surveys pose different questions, but it appears that both specialists and aides may be playing a more important role today.

There was a small but consistent trend across grades toward lesser availability of "other professionals," student teachers, and resource teachers. For example, 45 percent of the second-grade teachers, 48 percent of the fourth-grade teachers, and 51 percent of the sixth-grade teachers reported that resource teachers were *not* available. There was a decline over grades in remedial reading teachers, paraprofessionals, parents or volunteers, and older students. For example, 43 percent of the second-grade teachers reported the frequent availability of a remedial reading teacher, while only 28 percent of the sixth-grade teachers reported such availability. Similarly, 37 percent of the second-grade teachers and 25 percent of the sixth-grade teachers reported the frequent availability of a paraprofessional or teacher's aide.

These results show a tendency to place professional personnel resources in the lower elementary grades. One might speculate that the job of the second-grade teacher is considered to be more challenging, an attitude not uncommonly voiced by school personnel. Teachers and principals frequently seemed to suggest that younger children were more difficult to "manage," that they were less capable of working independently, and that they required more individual attention. Such statements conflict, or so it seems, with the opinion that individual differences are greater at the later grades (e.g., Harris & Sipay, 1975; Bond & Tinker, 1967).

There were a few noticeable effects of urbanization and geographic region of the country on availability of support personnel. Reading teachers were more available in the Northeast. Only 14 percent of the teachers from the Northeast reported that a remedial reading teacher was not available, about half the percentage in the other three regions. Paraprofessionals and aides were more common in large cities; 42 percent of the urban teachers reported that aides were frequently available, compared to 28 percent of teachers in other areas. Parents and/or volunteers were more available in the West. Twelve percent of the Western teachers reported that parent/volunteers were frequently available. By comparison, in the Northeast only 5 percent of the teachers reported that parent/volunteers were frequently available and 72 percent reported that they were not available at all.

Class Characteristics

Class Size

Class size is considered an important factor in organization for instruction. The questionnaire defined a class as "any instructional group that is exposed to a common set of materials, personnel and/or services, however large and extensive that set might be, and that can sensibly be treated as a group in terms of its general characteristics." This definition suggests that a class is an "instructional unit," concerned with more than attendance records and homeroom responsibilities.

Table 5-2 presents the class size data for compensatory classes. Class size increased with grade, especially from fourth to sixth grade, and graded classes were smaller than ungraded classes.

One might expect to find a lower teacher-pupil ratio in programs specifically designated to provide reading instruction to children who are not achieving in this area. However, the average class size for compensatory reading programs does not appear substantially different from regular classrooms. Class size was remarkably constant in all regions of the country, and in urban areas compared to rural areas. These findings are sharply discrepant from the data reported in the NIE (1976b) survey of compensatory programs, which showed average class sizes of eight students in

Table 5-2
Average Compensatory Class Size by Grade

	m	s.d.	n
Overall	28.2	13.9	1753
Graded:			
Second Grade	26.8	10.1	643
Fourth Grade	27.5	11.6	605
Sixth Grade	30.7	22.0	428
Ungraded	31.7	17.9	77

compensatory reading programs. We cannot tell whether this discrepancy reflects a difference in the way the question was posed, or a change in the organizational management of compensatory programs.

Number of Pupils per Teacher

Teachers were asked to report the total number of pupils who received reading instruction from them. Results are shown in Table 5-3. Reading groups were noticeably smaller than overall class size. At all grades a compensatory reading teacher was most likely to be responsible for the reading instruction of three to eight pupils. The next most common report was groups of 21 to 26 pupils. These reading group sizes were still about double those reported in the NIE (1976b) survey.

The number of questionnaires from regular teachers was too small for a trustworthy comparison. However, the average number of pupils taught reading in regular classrooms was 30.4, substantially greater than the average of 19.7 for compensatory programs. These data suggest that teachers in compensatory reading programs provided reading instruction for a small number of pupils.

We thought it would be interesting to examine the relation between number of students taught and teacher characteristics such as number of years of experience and special training in reading. In compensatory classes, there was a steady increase in the number of students with the teachers' years of experience, but the actual magnitude of the increase was small. The average number of pupils for a teacher with a single year of experience was 18.2, whereas the average for a teacher with more than twenty years was 20.5. Teachers with special reading training saw an average of 20.6 students, while those without such training saw only 18.2 students.

There were no consistent effects of geographical region or degree of urbanization on the number of pupils taught by compensatory reading teachers.

Grouping

Size of Reading Groups

Teachers were asked to describe the typical in-class reading group arrangements, with the results shown in Table 5-4. An adult working with a group of two to ten children was the predominant grouping pattern reported by teachers in compensatory reading programs. This organization

Table 5-3
Number of Pupils Taught per Teacher
in Compensatory Programs
(Percentage of Teachers Reporting at Selected Ranges)

Pupils per Teacher	GRADE			
	Second (n=657)	Fourth (n=622)	Sixth (n=449)	Ungraded (n=83)
Average Distribution	18.0	19.2	20.6	31.0
0- 2	2	1	1	1
3- 8	24	22	23	5
9-14	19	17	13	17
15-20	14	13	13	12
21-26	20	21	22	19
27-32	15	18	16	12
33-39	3	5	7	7
40 >	3	3	5	27

Table 5-4
Percentage of Teachers Reporting Frequency of Grouping Arrangements

Grouping Arrangement	Second (n=591 to 644)				Fourth (n=555 to 599)				Sixth (n=407 to 435)				Ungraded (n=75 to 81)			
	A	F	O	R	A	F	O	R	A	F	O	R	A	F	O	R
1 Adult and 1 Student	9	43	39	9	6	41	41	12	7	40	41	12	16	56	23	5
1 Adult and 2 to 10 Students	52	39	6	3	33	45	14	8	23	45	20	12	52	37	6	5
1 Adult and 10 to 20 Students	10	16	18	56	12	23	21	44	8	25	23	44	4	11	11	75
1 Adult and 20 or more Students	16	17	20	57	7	23	22	48	8	25	20	47	3	9	12	76

A = All the time   F = Frequently   O = Occasionally   R = Rarely

reflects the attitude that individual differences are best met by favorable adult-student ratios. Small group instruction was especially popular at second grade, and though it declined substantially over the grades, it was still fairly common at intermediate grades. Interestingly, second-grade teachers were also more likely to say that they worked with groups of 20 or more students "all the time" than were teachers at any other grade level.

The data from ungraded classes is atypical, especially in the use of groups of 10 or more students. Three quarters of the ungraded teachers stated that they only "rarely or never" worked with groups as large as ten; only about half the graded teachers made such a statement. This result fits with other findings to the effect that the ungraded classes were unusual.

Criteria for Grouping

Teachers were asked the extent to which they relied on selected criteria—reading grade level, specific skill deficiencies, shared interests, or specific projects—as a basis for forming instructional groups. The responses are summarized in Table 5-5.

Reading grade level was most commonly cited as a basis for creation of reading groups. This result fits the observation of Austin and Morrison

Table 5-5

Percentage of Teachers Reporting Selected Criteria for Forming Reading Groups

GRADE

Criterion	Second (n = 664)					Fourth (n = 630)					Sixth (n = 456)					Ungraded (n = 83)				
	F	O	R	N	N/R	F	O	R	N	N/R	F	O	R	N	N/R	F	O	R	N	N/R
Specific skill deficiencies	58	25	3	2	12	50	29	4	2	14	43	31	7	13	16	65	16	4	1	15
Shared interests	19	35	19	12	15	19	39	16	10	17	22	39	14	8	18	17	39	16	8	21
Specific projects	15	38	20	11	16	19	38	18	8	18	20	37	16	10	17	16	21	24	15	25
Reading grade level	69	16	3	2	10	64	16	3	3	13	59	18	6	3	13	63	12	5	6	15

F = Frequently   O = Occasionally   R = Rarely   N = Never   N/R = No Response

(1963): "With few exceptions . . . children were placed in groups according to reading ability . . ." (p. 76). Grouping children on the basis of specific skill deficiencies was the next most common practice, especially in ungraded classes. The widespread use of specific skill groupings would seem a reflection of the greater flexibility that one might anticipate in ungraded classrooms. Both grade level and skill deficiency as bases for grouping tended to diminish from second through sixth grade.

Shared interests and specific projects tended to serve "occasionally" as a basis for forming groups. This was true for graded as well as ungraded classes. One might have anticipated greater use of these criteria for grouping by ungraded teachers, since these criteria afford greater flexibility, but this was not observed. There was a noticeable tendency for upper grade teachers to report the use of these criteria.

Most teachers reported the use of all four grouping criteria to some extent. Only one in six teachers stated that they "never" used one or another of the criteria. These findings suggest that the frequently voiced admonition that teachers should maintain flexibility in grouping has been heard; even if reading level was most common, other criteria were also acknowledged as appropriate.

Teachers tended to resort to a "skill oriented" rationale for grouping. Though shared interests and specific projects can be effectively used for developing skills, many teachers may see these as more appropriate for extending interests and for fostering interpersonal interaction among students. These responses probably reflected the preservice and inservice programs to which they have been exposed, which likely placed emphasis on accountability and achievement test scores.

We carried out an analysis to see if there was a relation between the total number of pupils and the criteria used for grouping reported by teachers. Perhaps those teachers who relied on flexible grouping patterns (e.g., based on skill deficiency, interest, or special projects) had fewer students with which to deal. However, no relationship nor trend was found. The number of reading pupils per compensatory teacher remained constant (about 20) across grouping procedures. Neither was there any detectable relationship between the class size and the basis of grouping.

Frequency of Group Change

Teachers were asked about the extent to which changes were made in the composition of the reading groups, with the results shown in Table 5-6. Most teachers reported that they rarely changed the composition of the group. Only a third of the teachers said that they changed the reading group once a month or more often. These results are consistent with other findings (Groff, 1962; Hawkins, 1966; Austin & Morrison, 1963). For instance, Hawkins (1966) reported that 41 percent of the teachers in his study made *no* group changes during fourteen weeks. Nine percent of his

Table 5-6
Frequency of Change in Reading Group Composition
(Percentage of Teachers Marking Selected Categories)

Frequency	GRADE			
	Second (n=591)	Fourth (n=532)	Sixth (n=393)	Ungraded (n=69)
Daily	8	6	6	6
Weekly	4	8	9	3
Bi-weekly	3	6	6	7
Monthly	20	15	20	22
Rarely	45	45	39	33
Other	20	20	20	29

teachers made changes once a week. These percentages are virtually identical with those in the ETS survey. Hawkins maintained that teachers did not have clear reasons for instructional group changes: "The eight teachers [in the study] could not identify specifically the particular strengths or weaknesses that would make a reading group change instrumental in the child's progress" (p. 50). He concluded that the teachers could benefit from specific guidance about decision-making in constituting reading groups. We suspect that the conclusion holds for the ETS survey as well.

Scheduling

The final portion of this chapter deals with the scheduling of compensatory reading classes—length of instructional period, number of instructional periods per week, and total amount of instructional time per week.

Length of Instructional Period

Teachers were asked the amount of time they allotted to each instructional period. Table 5-7 summarizes their responses. Teachers arranged for half-hour instructional periods, on the average, at all grades. However, the

Table 5-7
Teachers' Judgments about Minutes per Instructional Period

Minutes	GRADE			
	Second (n=655)	Fourth (n=616)	Sixth (n=453)	Ungraded (n=82)
Average distribution in minutes	31.6	33.1	33.8	31.8
(Standard deviation)	(22.5)	(21.2)	(19.8)	(19.0)
1 - 15	22	24	25	13
16 - 30	38	27	17	46
31 - 40	16	12	14	15
41 - 50	8	14	25	15
51 - 60	6	14	13	6
61 - 75	2	4	4	1
76 - 90	5	4	1	0
91 or more	3	1	1	4

constancy in the average over grades obscures the changes in the distribution of time from one grade to the next. The modal length shifted from a half-hour in second and fourth grade to the "50-minute hour" at sixth grade. A quarter of the second-grade teachers reported periods longer than 40 minutes, whereas by sixth grade, almost half the teachers indicated reading sessions of this length. There was considerable uniformity in the length of instructional periods in ungraded classes, where almost half of the teachers reported instructional periods of 16 to 30 minutes.

Average number of minutes per instructional period was examined as a function of urbanization and region of the country. As a matter of fact,

Pikulski and Kirsch

the averages differ by less than two minutes. Compensatory instructional periods were more or less the same regardless of whether the school was in an urban, suburban, or rural setting and regardless of the region of the country.

Number of Instructional Periods

Teachers' estimates of the number of instructional periods scheduled each week for compensatory reading instruction is summarized in Table 5-8. Compensatory reading classes were generally scheduled four or five times per week. The trend toward more sessions per week in second grade was balanced with the fact that these sessions tend to be shorter (Table 5-7). Ungraded classes tended toward relatively fewer sessions per week than graded classes. The average number of periods per week in compensatory classrooms, 4.7, corresponded closely to the average of 5.0 for regular programs.

There was no effect of geographical region or urbanization on the number of instructional periods. When averages for various geographical regions and for urban, suburban, and rural areas were inspected, they all fell in the range between 4.6 and 4.7.

Total Instructional Time

Several studies (Harris & Serwer, 1966; Wiley & Harnischfeger, 1974; Guthrie, Martuza, & Seifert, 1976; McDonald & Elias, 1976) have shown a relationship between instructional time and reading achievement. In the

Table 5-8
Number of Reading Instructional Periods per Week
(Percentage of Teachers Marking each Category)

Number of Sessions per Week	GRADE			
	Second (n=655)	Fourth (n=618)	Sixth (n=453)	Ungraded (n=83)
1	1	1	1	1
2 - 3	5	10	14	22
4 - 5	64	78	78	67
6 or more	30	11	7	10

ETS survey, total time was estimated from the teachers' judgments of length and frequency of instructional periods. This estimation suggested that compensatory students received approximately 168 minutes (2.8 hours) of reading instruction per week. This is less than the nine hours per week that Gray and Rogers (1956) recommended for the primary grades, and even less than the five hours they recommended for the intermediate grades. The time allotments are also less than those reported by Ramsey (1967) who found a range from 60 minutes per day of reading instruction in grade one to 50 minutes in grade eight.

Part of the difference in results between the Ramsey study and the present survey may be due to the interpretation of instructional time. Harris and Serwer (1966), for example, distinguish between total reading time, supplemental reading time, and reading time. The wide variation in estimates of instructional time in the present survey—8 minutes to 700 minutes—also suggests that instructional time may be interpreted in a variety of ways by the teachers.

Scheduling of Reading Classes

Teachers, asked when reading was taught, generally said that it was scheduled in the morning. Only about ten percent reported that they varied the time of day when reading was taught. There were slight changes with grade. Eighty-eight percent of the second-grade and ungraded teachers taught reading in the morning, compared to 78 percent of the sixth-grade teachers.

Reading classes not held in the morning were scheduled during the afternoon hours of the regular day. Virtually no compensatory reading classes were held before or after the regular school day; only seven out of 1523 teachers in the sample reported otherwise.

These results are not surprising. Most elementary teachers and principals seem to agree that reading instruction should take place during the morning, because reading—the most important instructional activity in the elementary school—should be taught when children are most alert and attentive.

Special Scheduling for Compensatory Programs

Teachers were asked whether they thought that compensatory reading classes took the place of "regular" (non-compensatory) reading classes, or replaced some other regular school activity. Compensatory reading instruction usually replaced regular reading instruction according to two-thirds of the graded teachers. However, another arrangement that occurred with some frequency was for compensatory reading instruction to be held during the regular school day in place of some other scheduled activity. This event was reported less often in graded classes than in ungraded ones (Table 5-9). Compensatory reading instruction replaced seat work and

Pikulski and Kirsch

Table 5-9

Replacement of Other Activities by Compensatory Reading Instruction
(Percentage of Teachers Reporting Replacement in each Activity)

Activity Replaced	GRADE			
	Second (n=664)	Fourth (n=630)	Sixth (n=456)	Ungraded (n=83)
Social Studies	14	13	11	34
Science	12	11	9	22
Mathematics	4	6	6	8
Foreign Language	2	2	3	1
Language Arts	11	10	11	28
Physical Education	6	2	2	7
Art	9	6	4	11
Music	6	5	4	8
Seat work and study time	23	21	15	46

study time, social studies, language arts, and science. Less likely to be interrupted were mathematics, art, music, and physical education. There are slight grade trends that make sense, given the typical variations in curriculum from second through sixth grade. The ungraded classes are quite atypical. However, the overall pattern is remarkably similar to that reported in the NIE (1976b) survey.

The tendency for compensatory reading to replace other activities, especially in ungraded classes, may reflect the opinion that children should not be put into situations beyond their capability for success. This interpretation is consistent with the finding that the activities replaced are most dependent on reading skills (social studies, language arts, science). Mathematics, art, music, and physical education are less likely to be eliminated. Seat work and study time are general terms describing vague activities, and the assignment of this time to reading instruction is a measure of the teacher's sense of the priority to be assigned to reading.

Summary

If we take the liberty of ignoring a few exceptions, the following picture emerges as the most common organization for instruction in compensatory reading classes in the early 1970s:

The typical student attends a school that is graded. He is in the compensatory reading program because his reading level is depressed; teacher referral was probably the reason for which he was referred to the special reading program. His teacher has the services of a reading specialist available frequently or occasionally. Professionals like counselors and psychologists are occasionally or rarely available. Paraprofessionals or aides are either frequently available or not available at all. Parents, other volunteers, student teachers, media specialists, or older students are seldom present in the classroom.

There are about 28 other students in the class, and the teacher is responsible for the reading instruction for either a small (3 to 8 students) or large (21 to 26) group. The student receives reading instruction in a group of three to ten pupils, and it is not unlikely for him to receive one-to-one tutorial help. He was probably placed in a specific reading group on the basis of his reading level, and once placed in a group, it is not likely that he will be moved to another group. He is scheduled to receive compensatory reading instruction once a day, five times a week for 16 to 30 minutes. This compensatory reading instruction is regularly scheduled every morning, and actually replaces "regular" reading.

In general, traditional organizational schemes were typical of compensatory classrooms and schools. However, some encouraging trends emerged from the data, which run counter to the basic traditionalism. Teachers showed some awareness of individual differences in arranging for small-group activities and in organizing students according to specific needs and interests. It was also noteworthy that more than 60 percent of the teachers reported that specialized reading personnel were frequently or occasionally available.

The data from this survey do not speak directly to the question of whether reading achievement is influenced by classroom organization. Looking to other studies, we are hard pressed to find evidence supporting any such relations. Organization for reading instruction may be idiosyncratic and unpredictable. It may reflect diverse traditions or even whimsy. The data from this survey do not provide altogether clear answers to these questions. However, it seems to us that the conclusion of Austin and Morrison (1963, pp. 239-242) from their survey of administrators in regular schools holds as well for schools with compensatory programs—authority for organizational decisions is diffuse and poorly defined. Whether this feature of school organization influences the effectiveness of compensatory programs remains unanswered from the present survey.

Chapter 6

Instructional Procedures

Nancy Howlett
Sam Weintraub
State University of New York at Buffalo

This chapter presents and interprets the findings on instructional procedures reported by teachers responding to the Educational Testing Service (ETS) survey. The first section analyzes data from all compensatory classes. The second section emphasizes data from subgroups of teachers who relied primarily on one single instructional approach. It should be kept in mind that teachers were describing compensatory reading classes in which students read below the norm for their age group.

Instruction in Compensatory Classrooms

Approaches

When asked what approach they relied upon to teach reading, basal techniques were by far the most common choice for compensatory programs (Table 6-1). Individual teachers generally used more than one approach. For example a second-grade teacher might check both a basal and a total phonics program as "Extensively Used," so that the percentages total more than 100 at each grade level. Although basals remained the most widely used instructional tool, there was a trend toward greater use of individualized methods in particular.

Few teachers at any grade level reported much use of nonstandard orthography, words in color, or technological devices. For example, only 23 (1.3 percent) teachers said that they used nonstandard orthography extensively.

Table 6-2 combines the categories of Extensive and Some and therefore gives a more complete picture of instructional approaches. The high non-response rate of the sixth-grade teachers deserves notice because it

Table 6-1
Percentage of Teachers Reporting Extensive Use
of Selected Instructional Approaches

Approach	GRADE		
	Second (n=664)	Fourth (n=630)	Sixth (n=456)
Basal	67	61	46
Total Phonics	33	17	9
Supplemental Phonics	29	21	8
Language Experience	27	29	26
Individualized	24	31	36
Programmed	21	15	21
Linguistic	16	14	11

reflects on the other responses. These data again show the great reliance on the basal approach. The language experience approach was also used widely at all levels, with few teachers reporting that they never used it.

Total phonics programs were used to some extent in second grade but were much less common in sixth grade. Supplementary phonics programs were in fairly wide usage at all grade levels.

These findings are not especially surprising. They support conventional wisdom and previous surveys, notably *The First R* (Austin & Morrison, 1963). Regrettably, the programs were not precisely defined for or by the teachers. As noted in the case of the First-Grade Reading Study (Bond & Dykstra, 1967), definitions and procedures for particular approaches may vary markedly from place to place (Stauffer, 1970).

Major Goals

Teachers were asked the importance to them of several goals in teaching reading. Goals checked as of major importance by 80 percent or more of the teachers are listed in Table 6-3.

Table 6-2
Percentage of Teachers
Reporting Some Use of Selected Approaches

Approach	GRADE								
	Second (n=664)			Fourth (n=630)			Sixth (n=456)		
	Extensive or some	None	No Response	Extensive or some	None	No Response	Extensive or some	None	No Response
Basal	87	5	8	83	6	11	73	12	15
Language Experience	83	4	13	79	5	16	74	5	21
Supplemental Phonics	77	7	16	70	9	21	53	14	33
Linguistics	64	17	19	62	15	23	52	20	23
Total Phonics	64	24	12	48	29	23	33	36	31
Individualized	62	15	23	71	12	17	75	10	15

Table 6-3
Activities Rated as Major Goals in Teaching Reading
by 80 Percent or more Teachers

Goals	GRADE		
	Second (n=664)	Fourth (n=630)	Sixth (n=456)
Developing Comprehension	95	97	97
Improving Attitudes	92	92	93
Developing Listening Skills	92	81	71
Phonic/Structural Analysis	91	79	63
Developing Visual Discrimination	89	83	69
Developing Auditory Discrimination	85	68	52
Improving Self-Image	84	85	84
Learning Word Meanings	81	87	85
Reading Silently	81	76	77
Using Context Clues	81	81	84
Developing Study Skills	72	80	83
Improving Comprehension Rate	70	71	80

For all grade levels the development of comprehension skills and the improvement of attitudes toward reading were viewed as major goals. The major differences between the primary and intermediate grades occurred in the greater emphasis in the early grades on auditory discrimination, visual discrimination, phonics/structural analysis skills, listening skills, silent reading skills, and in the later grades on rate and study skills.

Time Spent on Various Activities

Teachers' responses to the question, "How much time does a typical pupil in your reading class spend in each of the following activities?" are reported in Table 6-4. At second grade, the largest number of teachers reported a great deal of time was spent on phonics and structural analysis skills. Phonics and word meanings were given most time by fourth-grade teachers. In the sixth grade, word meanings and silent reading were given priority.

In second grade there was a high correspondence between the percentage of teachers who reported phonics/structural analysis skills as major goals (91 percent) and the percentage who checked that their pupils spent a great deal of time on this activity (87 percent). At sixth grade, 77 percent of the teachers said that reading silently was a major goal, while 70 percent thought the typical pupil spent a great deal of time reading silently. These figures also indicate a relatively close correspondence between stated goals and time spent in reading. For other activities, the relationship between stated importance as a goal and time spent was not so obviously consistent. For example, "reading for enjoyment" was viewed as a major goal by about 77 percent of the teachers at each grade level, but less than half replied that a typical pupil spent a large amount of time on that activity. It is to be remembered that we are viewing compensatory classrooms only. In Chapter 9 the relation between goals and time allocation will be examined in some detail, and we shall see that there are some systematic correspondences.

Table 6-4
Percentage of Teachers Spending "A Great Deal"
of Time on Various Activities

Activity	GRADE		
	Second (n=664)	Fourth (n=630)	Sixth (n=456)
Phonic/Structural Analysis	87	68	51
Developing Sight Vocabulary	68	55	47
Learning Word Meanings	66	75	74
Reading Silently	64	65	70
Reading Aloud	63	42	33
Developing Visual Discrimination	61	40	30
Reading Enjoyment	45	46	48

Oral Reading

Two questions were asked about oral reading. Teachers judged how often a child had an opportunity to read aloud to the class. About 84 percent of the second-grade teachers, 73 percent of the fourth-grade teachers, and 59 percent of the sixth-grade teachers responded that the typical child read aloud "once a day" or "several times a week." The second question was "About how often does each child in your compensatory reading class have the opportunity to read aloud to you alone (or to another adult)?" About 70 percent of the second-grade teachers, 47 percent of the fourth-grade teachers, and 38 percent of the sixth-grade teachers reported that children read aloud to an adult several times a week or more often.

It appears that oral reading occurred with considerable frequency at all levels of the elementary school, even though not all teachers rated oral reading as a major goal (44 percent at second grade, 26 percent at fourth, and 22 percent at sixth). The questionnaire did not inquire about either the purpose or nature of the oral reading being done. Thus, it is possible to report only that frequent oral reading seems to be the mode.

Approaches to Reading Instruction

In this section we examine and compare the responses of teachers who relied extensively on a single instructional approach—basal, phonics, language experience, or individualized. The teachers in each group tend to be a "pure" sample of a particular approach. The maximum number of teachers at each grade for the different approaches is displayed in Table 6-5. The reader should keep in mind the small number of sixth-grade teachers in the phonics group and interpret percentages accordingly.

Major Goals

Teachers were asked to rate a list of activities in terms of their importance as goals in teaching reading. Two of these activities, developing comprehension and improving attitudes, were viewed as being of major importance by more than 90 percent of teachers at all grade levels.

Comprehension was identified as a major goal at all grade levels and for all approaches. A similar pattern occurred for improving attitudes. The phonics subgroup rated phonics and structural analysis as a more important goal than did teachers of other approaches, especially in the fourth and sixth grades. Language experience teachers gave phonics a lower rating, especially at the sixth grade.

In summary, only minimal differences appeared among the emphases given the goals when they are analyzed by approaches and/or by grade levels. The trend was for teachers to give similar responses at a given grade level, no matter what the reading approach. There was great similarity in how goals were viewed *across* approaches *in compensatory programs.*

Table 6-5
Number of Teachers Making "Extensive" Use
of a Single Approach at each Grade Level

Approach	GRADE		
	Second	Fourth	Sixth
Basal	203	193	114
Phonics	104	46	19
Language Experience	125	105	74
Individualized	136	176	160

Time on Activities

As noted earlier, teachers were asked "How much time does a typical pupil in your reading class spend in each of the following activities?" On the scale, 1 corresponded to "a great deal [of time]," 2 was "some time," and 3 was "little or no time."

Table 6-6 presents in summary form the relation between the instructional approaches and the teachers' judgments of activities in which there are major time expenditures, as defined by an average rating between 1.0 and 1.6 on the response scale.

The table reveals considerable similarities among the approaches. Teachers at all grades and in all approaches judged that vocabulary development and silent reading consumed a great deal of time. The questionnaire did not list comprehension as an activity. However, we suspect that the teachers in all approaches thought that comprehension was an important aspect of reading and that vocabulary and silent reading contributed to growth in comprehension.

Other activities on which a typical pupil spent a great deal of time in most grades and in all approaches included phonics and structural analysis skills, developing sight vocabulary, and reading for enjoyment.

Another activity which is important in the primary grades is oral reading. The second-grade teachers in all approaches judged oral reading to be an important activity, as expected. However, classrooms above the second grade using the individualized approach did less oral reading than in any other approach. At the sixth-grade level, the teachers of the phonics and language experience approaches showed that "a great deal" of time was spent on oral reading.

Table 6-6
Grade Levels with a Major Time Expenditure
for each Activity in each Approach

Activity	Basal (n=510)	Phonics (n=169)	Language Experience (n=304)	Individualized (n=472)
Phonics/Structural Analysis	2,4,6	2,4,6	2,4	2,4,6
Developing Visual Discrimination	2	2,4	2	2,4
Developing Sight Vocabulary	2,4	2,4,6	2,4,6	2,4,6
Learning Word Meanings	2,4,6	2,4,6	2,4,6	2,4,6
Reading Silently	2,4,6	2,4,6	2,4,6	2,4,6
Increasing Attention Span		4	2,4	2,4
Reading Aloud	2,4	2,4,6	2,4,6	2
Reading for Enjoyment	2,4	2,4,6	2,4,6	2,4,6
Matching Letters and Words		2	2	
Learning Letter Forms		2	2	

Visual discrimination consumed considerable time in second grade in every approach. Visual discrimination is thought to be a beginning reading activity and so is expected in the early primary grades. Because many of the teachers had compensatory classes, they were teaching beginning reading skills and hence the emphasis on visual discrimination. At fourth-grade level, teachers of the phonics and individual approaches also reported considerable time on visual discrimination. This was not true in the basal and language experience approaches. The other three activities in Table 6-6 vary somewhat from one approach to another, but with no clearcut pattern.

Overall, the activities reported by teachers of the various approaches were not very different. Most teachers in each of the four approaches reported that the following activities took "a great deal" of time: phonics and structural skills, developing sight vocabulary, learning word meanings, reading silently, and reading for enjoyment. In particular, phonics and structural analysis skills were the first ranked activities at second grade in all approaches, and among the first three activities in fourth grade in all approaches. All things considered, it would be difficult to differentiate the four approaches by the types of activities reported as most common in compensatory reading instruction.

Oral Reading

Two questions pertained to oral reading in the instructional setting. The first asked teachers to respond to the frequency with which children were given opportunities to read aloud to the class; the second asked about the frequency of opportunities to read aloud to the teacher or another adult. The results in Table 6-7 show that oral reading was more frequent at the primary level than the upper grade levels. Reading aloud to the class was more common in the basal, phonics, and language experience approaches than in individualized classes; reading aloud to an adult tended to be more common in individualized instruction than in the other approaches.

In general, these data show less reading aloud to the class as children progress through the grades. There was less reading aloud to the class and more frequent child-to-adult reading in individualized programs than in other programs. On the other hand, the basal approach tended to show less child-to-adult oral reading than did the others. Language experience and individualized approaches tend by their nature to encourage more one-to-one interaction, whereas the basal approach has more small group oriented instruction occurring. These generalizations fit compensatory programs just as well as regular programs.

Independent Reading and Library Work

Teachers were asked, "For a typical pupil in your compensatory reading program, about how much in-school time is devoted to each of the following reading or reading-related activities?" We are interested here specifically in time spent on independent reading and in-library reading. Respondents checked "none," "less than 1 hour per week," "between 1 and 4 hours per week," or "more than 1 hour a day." These responses, converted to appropriate minutes per week, are shown in Table 6-8.

The most striking result of this analysis was that students in the individualized approach spent much more time in independent reading than in any other approach. These results are consistent with the notion that an important component of the individualized program is independent reading. By sixth grade, this difference became even sharper, and the individualized teachers reported that the students spent almost 20 minutes more a week on independent reading than in any other approach.

In Table 6-9 the mean number of minutes per week spent in library activities is presented. At most grades and approaches, about an hour per week was devoted to library work. At second grade, teachers in the individualized approach gave the greatest amount of time to library work. At fourth grade, the individualized and phonics approach teachers reported virtually identical times. By sixth grade, there were no differences in approaches.

Table 6-7

Teacher Ratings of Frequency of Students' Oral Reading

[1 = at least once a day   2 = Several times a week, but not daily
3 = about once a week   4 = less than once a week but regularly]

	GRADE								
	Second			Fourth			Sixth		
	Mean	s.d.	n	Mean	s.d.	n	Mean	s.d.	n
Reading aloud to the class									
Approach									
Basal	1.70	.88	203	2.16	.97	191	2.51	1.08	113
Phonics	1.61	.91	102	2.15	1.01	46	1.90	1.05	19
Language Experience	1.74	.14	125	2.18	1.05	104	2.22	1.04	73
Individualized	2.24	.41	135	2.55	1.33	176	3.01	1.31	158
Reading aloud to an adult									
Approach									
Basal	2.64	1.48	203	3.43	1.42	191	3.59	1.37	113
Phonics	2.20	1.31	102	2.98	1.31	46	2.63	1.38	19
Language Experience	2.32	1.31	124	2.70	1.41	103	3.05	1.44	74
Individualized	1.85	1.05	135	2.52	1.18	174	2.93	1.23	158

Table 6-8
Average Minutes per Week Spent in Independent Reading

| | GRADE | | | | | | | | | | |
| Approach | Second | | | Fourth | | | Sixth | | |
	Minutes	s.d.	n	Minutes	s.d.	n	Minutes	s.d.	n
Basal	106	71	202	102	72	186	120	71	112
Phonics	107	68	102	123	83	45	102	104	19
Language Experience	117	82	122	100	74	103	109	71	73
Individu- alized	124	74	130	131	82	166	138	96	156

Table 6-9
Average Minutes per Week Spent in Library Activities

Approach	Second			Fourth			Sixth		
	Minutes	s.d.	n	Minutes	s.d.	n	Minutes	s.d.	n
Basal	60	56	198	60	59	188	77	69	112
Phonics	55	51	99	73	79	46	77	60	18
Language Experience	68	70	120	61	54	103	75	74	73
Individu-alized	74	60	130	72	73	168	72	70	155

Grouping

As noted in Chapter 5, grouping may affect instruction. Results on instructional grouping within the basal, phonics, language experience, and individualized approaches are reported here.

Table 6-10 shows teachers' answers to the question: "How often do the following instructional groups operate in the course of your teaching of compensatory reading?" Regardless of the approach or grade, teachers used a grouping pattern in which the adult met with a group of between two and ten children. The data show some evidence of relatively smaller grouping patterns in individualized approaches, but even here the effects were slight.

To the question, ". . . about how frequently does the composition of the group change?" teachers gave the responses in Table 6-11. Here again, the most remarkable outcome was the small effect of the instructional approach on frequency of group change. Indeed, no real differences appeared in terms of frequency of group change.

Teachers were asked to indicate how often they used each of the following criteria in forming groups: "reading grade level," "specific skill deficiencies," "shared interests," and "special projects" (Table 6-12). The most striking effect in this table is the relatively marked emphasis on using reading grade level and specific skill deficiencies to form groups. These two approaches were used more frequently than shared interests or special projects in all approaches and grades. The average response for the phonic, language experience, and individualized teachers at each grade was that they used interests and projects "occasionally" in forming groups. The basal teachers reported that they used these criteria less often than the teachers of the other approaches.

Summary

A brief overview of the instructional practices may provide a total picture in some perspective. The typical second grade compensatory classroom teacher uses a basal reader. In addition, she may follow a language experience approach with supplementary phonics. The major goals for her instructional program are to develop comprehension, improve attitudes toward reading, develop listening skills, and teach phonics/ structural analysis skills. In addition, visual and auditory discrimination are seen as important objectives. There is a rough match between these goals and time expenditures.

Children reading aloud to the class is a daily occurrence. Instruction occurs in small groups of two to ten children, who have been placed in the group on the basis of reading grade level. The composition of these groups rarely changes—"once a blue jay always a blue jay" (Austin & Morrison, 1963, p. 79).

Table 6-10

Rated Frequency of Instructional Arrangements for Different Approaches to Teaching Reading

[1 = All the time   2 = Frequently   3 = Occasionally   4 = Rarely or Never]

Grouping	Second				Fourth				Sixth			
	Basal (N=185 to 202)	Phonic (N=92 to 100)	Lang. Exper. (N=114 to 123)	Indiv. (N=114 to 133)	Basal (N=173 to 187)	Phonic (N=41 to 45)	Lang. Exper. (N=91 to 101)	Indiv. (N=154 to 173)	Basal (N=100 to 110)	Phonic (N=15 to 19)	Lang. Exper. (N=69 to 73)	Indiv. (N=140 to 154)
1 Adult to 1 Student	2.7	2.6	2.5	2.0	2.9	2.7	2.6	2.3	2.9	2.4	2.6	2.3
1 Adult, 2-10 Students	1.6	1.5	1.6	1.7	2.0	1.9	2.0	2.0	2.3	2.0	2.3	2.0
1 Adult, 11-20 Students	3.2	3.0	3.1	3.3	2.8	3.1	2.9	3.1	2.8	3.0	2.9	3.2
1 Adult, over 20 Students	3.4	3.0	3.1	3.4	3.0	3.0	2.9	3.4	2.8	3.3	2.8	3.3
Individual Indep. Work	2.2	2.1	2.2	1.9	2.3	2.3	2.1	1.9	2.3	2.1	2.2	2.0
Pupil Teams	2.8	2.8	2.6	2.5	2.9	2.7	2.7	2.5	2.9	2.7	2.8	2.6

Howlett and Weintraub

Table 6-11
Average Frequency of Change in Group by Approach and Grade
[1 = Daily   2 = Weekly   3 = Bi-weekly   4 = Monthly   5 = Rarely]

| Approach | GRADE | | | | | |
| | Second | | Fourth | | Sixth | |
	m	n	m	n	m	n
Basal	4.6	187	4.7	161	4.6	98
Phonic	4.7	93	4.7	41	3.8	18
Language Experience	4.4	113	4.5	89	4.4	63
Individualized	4.2	118	4.0	150	4.3	139

Fourth and sixth grade compensatory classroom teachers do things about the same as their primary level colleagues with regard to instructional approach, goals, and time expenditures. A visitor to a fourth grade would likely encounter a child reading orally to the class on almost any day of the week. The chances are that he would hear some children reading orally in sixth grade also, although with a bit less frequency than in the fourth. At both of these grade levels, our visitor would probably come upon a child reading orally to the teacher or some other adult in a one-to-one situation. Silent reading would be more commonly observed than in second grade. Most of his observations would be made of children in small groups of two to ten who are together because of similarity in test scores. He would see some groups formed on the basis of specific skill deficiency or common interests.

What features would our hypothetical visitor note if he asked to see compensatory classrooms emphasizing particular approaches to reading? Many similarities would be noted. He would be struck with the sameness of the goals in different approaches. He would find some differences in the amount of time devoted to various activities. In the basal classrooms, for example, less time would be devoted to activities for increasing attention span at second and fourth grades than in other approaches. He would find less time spent in the basal classrooms on reading for enjoyment. Somewhat surprisingly, he would note that developing sight vocabulary is not important in the basal programs but that it is in the others.

In general, our visitor would find that teachers of individualized approach classrooms tend to show the sharpest distinctions with the

Table 6-12
Frequency with which Certain Criteria Are Used for Organizing Groups by Grade and Approach
[1 = Frequently   2 = Occasionally   3 = Rarely   4 = Never]

	GRADE											
	Second				Fourth				Sixth			
					Approach							
Grouping	Basal (N=177 to 187)	Phonic (N=88 to 97)	Lang. Exper. (N=111 to 115)	Indiv. (N=108 to 118)	Basal (N=161 to 175)	Phonic (N=38 to 42)	Lang. Exper. (N=90 to 93)	Indiv. (N=143 to 149)	Basal (N=92 to 102)	Phonic (N=15 to 17)	Lang. Exper. (N=64 to 66)	Indiv. (N=131 to 134)
Reading												
Grade Level	1.2	1.2	1.3	1.5	1.3	1.3	1.3	1.5	1.3	1.2	1.4	1.7
Specific Skill												
Deficiency	1.6	1.3	1.3	1.4	1.7	1.5	1.4	1.4	1.8	1.3	1.6	1.5
Shared												
Interests	2.6	2.3	2.0	2.0	2.4	2.1	2.1	2.0	2.4	1.8	2.0	1.9
Special												
Projects	2.5	2.4	2.1	2.1	2.3	2.2	2.0	2.0	2.4	2.2	2.0	2.0

other approaches. The most dramatic difference would be the replacement of oral reading to the class with child-to-teacher, one-to-one oral reading. There would be more time spent on independent reading. At second and fourth grades, the guest would witness more time spent in library activities than in other approaches.

There seem to be greater differences *within* approaches than *between* them. Several factors may contribute to this finding. First is the teacher's individual style. The teacher unquestionably determines the specific emphasis within an instructional procedure. Not only do teachers' abilities and personalities influence what happens within a given approach, their "definitions" of what constitutes a given approach vary. The similarities among approaches also reflect a trend toward eclecticism in both the background and educational training of teachers, and in the thinking of the teachers themselves. This eclecticism obscures sharp distinctions. The blurring of differences may also reflect the type of classrooms sampled. In these classrooms, one deals primarily with children who read below average. Poor readers may call forth specific instructional practices, regardless of the approach used. Distinctiveness in approaches may be more marked in the general population, though we know of little evidence to support such a proposition.

Chapter 7

Selection and Use of Instructional Materials

Carol N. Dixon
University of California at Santa Barbara

The Educational Testing Service (ETS) Survey of Compensatory Reading Programs covered several matters related to the selection and use of instructional materials, including the responsibility for selecting materials, the degree of satisfaction with the way materials were selected, the use of non-text materials, and the relative popularity of text materials from different publishers. The teachers' and principals' responses to these questions are discussed in this chapter, and where appropriate, the data are related to grade level, urbanization, and geographic area.

The survey format is effective to the degree that the questions are effectively phrased, and certain of the items requesting information about teaching materials were ambiguous or provided ambiguous responses. For example, one of the answers available for the question "who selected the materials that you are currently using in your teaching of compensatory reading?" was "an individual who asked for your views; or a team or committee of which you were not a member but on which your views were represented." By combining the "individual" with the "committee or group" as equivalent ways of assigning responsibility, a potentially significant distinction was obscured.

Selection of Materials

Responsibility for Selection

Who decides what instructional materials to use in the classroom? An obvious and logical answer is "the teacher, of course." In a sense, it is true that the teacher does choose the instructional materials, for he distributes the materials that are actually used by the students. However, the teacher most often selects from a limited set of possibilities.

Schools provide varied amounts and kinds of materials from which to learn, and some communities are more open to experimentation and innovation in their schools than others. In school systems where individual teachers or teacher committees decide which approach and materials will be used, decisions may be reached as a result of previous success with certain materials, convictions based on professional reading literature or ideas gained through participation in workshops. Sometimes administrators make decisions in response to parental wishes, budgetary considerations or because they rely on the quality of one set of materials over another. (Tuinman, 1971, p. 3)

In addition to constraints which originate at the district or local school level, further restrictions on the availability of materials may come from state or federal sources. For example, the California State Constitution requires that all materials purchased with state funds be approved by State Department of Education committees for compliance with standards that are legal (e.g., absence of racial, religious, or sexual bias) and substantive (e.g., representative skills, materials quality).

Whatever factors influence the purchase of materials, the teacher ultimately decides whether they will be used or will remain on the shelf. Thus, for practical reasons, teachers should have a voice in the selection process to ensure that funds will not be wasted on unused materials.

The following question measured the teacher's input in the selection process: "Who selected the materials that you are currently using in your teaching of compensatory reading?" The teachers' responses are shown in Table 7-1. In general, selection of materials at all grades was most frequently a group decision, with or without the teacher's input. However, all five methods of determining responsibility for selection of materials received considerable use, and no one approach had overwhelming "popularity." When responsibility for selection of materials is compared by grade, a slight trend does emerge. When we compare responses in the first two categories with those in the last two, we see that teacher control over selection of materials increased by grade levels and in the ungraded classroom. One might speculate that this trend resulted from greater emphasis on content materials, less emphasis on reading series, and more individualized instruction in ungraded classes. As will be seen below, the trend toward more teacher control in the upper grades and in ungraded classes did parallel decreased emphasis on basal readers.

We looked at the relations between answers to the selection question and two teacher characteristics, reading training and years of experience. Teachers with reading training comprised 60 percent of those who reported sole responsibility for selection, 64 percent of those who voted as members of a committee, and 57 percent of those who provided a committee with input. Only half the teachers who said they had no input reported any reading training. Sixty-two percent of teachers who said "other" selection procedures were used had had some reading training. The nonresponse rate was about the same (6 to 7 percent) for teachers

Table 7-1

Selection of Reading Materials

(Percentage of Teachers Marking each Response)

Response	GRADE			
	Second (n=664)	Fourth (n=630)	Sixth (n=456)	Ungraded (n= 83)
Teacher	12	20	20	19
Teacher as Member of Committee	23	23	24	27
Committee with Teacher Input	22	16	17	16
Committee with no Teacher Input	28	22	23	14

with and without training. All in all, teachers who were active in the selection process were more likely to have had some reading training. The data also show that teachers who were active in the selection process were apt to have had more teaching experience. Teachers in the first two selection categories were more likely to have had 10 to 20 years of experience, while teachers marking the last two categories tended to have had 6 to 10 years of experience.

Unfortunately, principals were not asked directly about selection of materials. It would have been interesting to learn whether the principals' perceptions agreed with the teachers' and whether principals tended to rely on the better trained and more experienced teachers for selection of materials.

Responsibility for selection of materials was also examined in relation to urbanization and geographic location. Table 7-2 shows that teachers in urban areas were more likely to have a vote in selection than teachers in rural areas. This finding is somewhat surprising; one might expect that lower population density and smaller schools would lead to greater individual teacher input. However, lower population density may actually mean greater centralization of authority (for example, in the district office) and thus less teacher voice in the decision.

Dixon

Teachers in the West were considerably more likely to have a vote in the selection of materials than their counterparts in the Northeast, North Central, or Southern United States. The Western United States is characterized by greater physical distances between schools and more population mobility. The larger size of school districts promotes more individual autonomy and less centralization. Population mobility also tends to reduce community stability and to increase diversity within and between schools. Unfortunately, while this mobility may give teachers a greater voice in what they use for instruction, it may also be distressing to the children. The elementary student who moves through six different schools where each teacher has chosen his own instructional materials may be at a disadvantage.

Satisfaction with Materials

Since the results of the survey show that teachers often work with a collection of instructional materials not of their own choosing, considerable dissatisfaction might be expected. Teachers were asked: "How satisfied are you with the materials you are currently using in your teaching of compensatory reading?" It is true that "What satisfies one does not satisfy another" (Austin & Morrison, 1963, p. 65). Nonetheless, the most

Table 7-2

Selection of Materials as a Function
of Urbanization and Geographic Region
(Percentage of Teachers Marking each Response)

	RESPONSE				
	Teacher	Teacher in Committee	Committee with Teacher Input	Committee – No Teacher Input	n
Urbanization					
Urban	20	26	15	25	392
Suburban	19	24	22	24	663
Rural	17	24	21	29	504
Geographic Area					
Northeast	15	26	19	26	340
North Central	18	22	22	28	541
South	16	26	21	28	489
West	26	29	16	18	354

clearcut generalization from the data in Table 7-3 is that the majority of the teachers were happy with the instructional materials they were using. Some departures from this trend are worth noting. For instance, the responses indicate that teachers of ungraded classes were the most satisfied with the materials they were using. They also had the greatest control over the selection process. However, sixth-grade teachers were less satisfied than second-grade teachers, yet had a greater voice in the selection process. This may reflect less teacher satisfaction with materials available for use in the upper grades, independent of the manner in which the materials were selected.

Principals were not asked a directly parallel question about their satisfaction with instructional materials. However, they were asked: "Using your best professional judgment, rate each of the following characteristics for your school."

Three of the characteristics they were asked to consider were the quality and quantity of books, audiovisual aids, and equipment. The principals were overwhelmingly positive about the quality of books, audiovisual aids, and equipment available in their schools and only slightly less positive about the quantity of those materials available. They appeared to be happier with the materials at their disposal than with the human resources, such as the number of aides or nonprofessionals. The tone of the administrators' responses in *The First R* reflected a lack of appropriate

Table 7-3
Teacher Satisfaction with Materials
(Percentage of Teachers Marking each Response)

Response	GRADE			
	Second (n=654)	Fourth (n=622)	Sixth (n=453)	Ungraded (n=81)
Totally Satisfied	13	11	14	15
Satisfied in Major Aspects	64	66	57	77
Lukewarm	15	15	20	6
Dissatisfied in Major Aspects	7	8	8	2
Totally Dissatisfied	1	0	1	0

instructional materials, especially in less affluent school districts (Austin & Morrison, 1963, p. 65). State and federal funding programs have apparently been effective in improving the situation.

Instructional Materials

Nontext Materials Used

Results presented in Chapter 6 have shown that compensatory reading teachers used a variety of instructional approaches. It might be expected that there would also be variety in instructional materials. Teachers were asked about the materials they used in their classes. The results (Table 7-4)

Table 7-4
Use of Instructional Materials
(Percentage of Teachers Reporting "Sometimes" or "Often Use")

Materials	GRADE			
	Second (n=625 to 657)	Fourth (n=583 to 617)	Sixth (n=423 to 451)	Ungraded (n=75 to 82)
Textbooks other than Basals	90	88	78	70
Books other than Texts	95	96	98	97
Newspapers, Magazines	70	79	85	73
Teacher-Prepared Materials	99	98	96	93
Movies or Filmstrips	80	77	73	68
Slides and Transparencies	55	59	56	51
Tapes and Records	84	80	75	88
Video or TV Tapes	25	24	22	24
Games, Puzzles, Toys	94	88	74	91

make it possible to rank order the use of specific types of instructional materials. Teacher-prepared materials and books other than texts were the most popular, while video or TV tapes were the least used. In discussing the use of trade or library books to teach reading, Austin and Morrison (1963) found "47 percent in grades 1 through 3 and 54 percent in grades 4 through 6 indicate that reading is so taught to a 'moderate' degree" (p. 60). They also stated that "weekly newspapers and magazines, published by a variety of companies and graded in terms of difficulty, are fairly common among the school systems of the field study, although no great emphasis on using them as a teaching device was evident" (p. 62), and "audio-visual aids such as filmstrips and films . . . were also noted, although their use is hardly widespread" (p. 63). The results of the present survey suggest that all three types of materials have undergone significant growth in popularity during the past ten years, at least in compensatory classrooms.

On the other hand, Austin and Morrison also noted that "only 13 of the 51 systems visited reported that they had any kind of educational television programs related to reading or the language arts. . . . Budgetary considerations loomed large in any discussion of television in the classroom, for while some school systems were able to provide a set for every room, in other schools there was only one set for a floor" (p. 62-63). Apparently, there has been little change in this situation. Videotapes were the only materials marked as "unavailable" by a significant proportion (30 percent) of teachers in the present survey. A grade level trend appears, with second-grade teachers reporting greater use of materials other than basals than sixth-grade teachers. Only newspapers, magazines, and other periodicals received greater use at sixth grade than at second, a realistic reflection of the reading levels of periodical materials generally available to teachers. The use of fewer non-basal materials at sixth grade may reflect less time spent on teaching reading and more emphasis on "reading to learn."

Ninety-three percent of the teachers indicated that they had made some of the materials they were using. It is not surprising that teacher-made materials were so popular, given the emphasis on individualization of instruction and the ready availability of ditto machines. The survey also attempted to identify specific kinds of teacher-made materials (Table 7-5). Worksheets were by far the most common. To be sure, we cannot tell whether the worksheets were based on the suggestions from a basal manual, which some educators consider of dubious value (Veatch, Swicki, Elliott, Barnette, & Blakey, 1973) or were designed for the specific needs of their students.

Teacher-made charts, stories, etc., and tapes also received considerable use. Teacher-made filmstrips, slides, and motion pictures, which require more time, money, and technical expertise to produce, were seldom

Table 7-5
Teacher-Made Instructional Materials
(Percentage of Teachers Reporting Use)

Materials	GRADE			
	Second (n=664)	Fourth (n=630)	Sixth (n=456)	Ungraded (n=83)
Worksheets	93	87	85	92
Printed Stories, Poems, Essays	66	56	51	66
Transparencies for Overhead	37	38	34	31
Filmstrips	7	8	9	2
Slides	6	6	8	6
Motion Pictures	4	4	6	1
Charts	82	67	55	76
Tapes	45	43	38	61

reported. It is unfortunate that items such as flash cards, cartoons, puppets, and games were not included in the list, since they also are used in some reading classes. The substantial amount of teacher-made material may be an encouraging sign, insofar as it reflects a trend toward instruction designed to meet specific needs of a class.

Published Text Materials Used

The final question about selection and use of instructional materials concerned the nature of published reading materials. A number of publishers had more than one series available for elementary reading. The data reported only the use of materials from a particular publishing company, not the specific reading materials.

In Table 7-6, "major resource" and "supplemental material" responses have been combined to provide grade level comparisons. Ranking by

Table 7-6
Use of Published Text Materials
(Percentage of Teachers Reporting "Major" or "Supplemental Use")

Publisher	GRADE			
	Second (n=664)	Fourth (n=630)	Sixth (n=456)	Ungraded (n=83)
Scott Foresman	53	53	46	34
Harper & Row	29	19	21	12
Macmillan	30	21	21	20
American Book Company	19	18	18	14
Ginn and Company	46	34	29	21
Houghton-Mifflin	24	18	16	22
Lippincott	11	8	4	11
Allyn and Bacon	12	7	8	7
Holt, Rinehart and Winston	9	9	9	11
SRA	35	49	53	43
Harcourt Brace and World	6	6	7	11
Open Court	12	6	10	23
ita	6	2	4	0
Merrill Linguistics	14	23	20	23

publisher shows that materials produced by Scott Foresman, SRA, and Ginn were most commonly used in compensatory reading classes. Answers to preceding questions had indicated less use of non-basal and teacher-made materials as grade level increased. This might have suggested greater reliance on published reading texts in the upper grades. However, the trend found is one of less use of publishers' reading text materials by sixth grade, with the exception of SRA and Merrill-Linguistic materials which were used more in sixth grade than they were at second. The teachers in the later grades apparently made less use of reading materials of any sort.

The reply to this question made it possible to determine not only how "popular" certain publishers were but also how many teachers tended to rely on a single publisher's materials for reading instruction. In 1963, Austin and Morrison found that "64 percent of the 795 respondents indicated that their system in grades 1 through 3 relied 'predominantly' or 'exclusively' on a single basal series as the chief tool of instruction. . . . Basal readers receive almost the same emphasis in the intermediate grades with over 60 percent reporting 'predominant' or 'exclusive' use of a single series . . ." (p. 54). The present survey revealed a different picture ten years later in compensatory classrooms. Only 24 percent of the 1750 teachers indicated use of a single source of published materials for instructional purposes. There was no significant difference between grade levels in the trend toward greater variety.

Summary

This chapter has discussed results of the ETS compensatory reading survey about the selection and use of materials. The most significant finding was the tendency for teachers of compensatory reading to use a wide variety of instructional approaches and materials. In contrast to previous studies, compensatory reading teachers reported reduced reliance on basal readers and on use of a single text as their total reading program. No one approach or publisher's materials was used to the exclusion of others, although basal readers and language experience were clearly the most popular instructional approaches. Overall, the questions dealing with use of specific instructional materials show a broad range of use, with no one material or publisher being used exclusively. Austin and Morrison had concluded that of the multitude of reading materials published, the "basal readers with their accompanying manuals and workbooks are used more extensively than any other materials. Indeed, in a good many classes they are utilized as the *only* tools of instruction" (p. 69). Although basals remain the most popular material, it appears that they were seldom the only materials reported in this survey. Compensatory reading teachers were making extensive use of a broad spectrum of instructional materials, including a wide variety of commercial and teacher-made non-basal materials as they attempted to meet the needs of their students.

The data show that though many teachers felt they did not have a vote in the selection of materials they were to use, teachers and principals were for the most part satisfied with the materials available.

In conclusion, "however the decisions are arrived at, whatever approaches, methods, or materials used, it is important to remember that the teaching of reading can be successful with any of the approaches . . . or a combination of them." (Tuinman, 1971, p. 3) The crucial issue is not *what* is used, but rather how. The prime concern continues to be what actually happens in the classroom once the methods and materials have been chosen.

Chapter 8

Teacher Attitudes, Purposes, Practices, and Outcomes

Priscilla A. Drum
University of California at Santa Barbara
Robert C. Calfee
Stanford University

The previous chapters have examined teacher responses to individual questions. It is somewhat difficult to detect patterns over the set of 260 items. How is the answer on one item related to answers on other items? For instance, we learn that 49 percent of the 664 second grade teachers rated "matching letters or words" as a major goal, while only 20 percent rated "developing library skills" as a major goal. However, we don't learn the extent to which some teachers shared the two responses as common goals.

In this chapter, we will organize responses to questions about attitudes, goals, and practices for reading instruction in order to seek a structure which will make the disparate responses more meaningful.

Certain multiple-item questions in the questionnaire appear to have a natural structure. For instance:

How much time does a typical pupil in your compensatory reading class spend in each of the following types of activity?
1. Improving motor abilities related to reading
2. Increasing attention span
3. Developing visual discrimination
4. Matching letters or words
5. Learning letter forms
6. Developing a sight vocabulary
7. Learning word meanings
8. Phonic and/or structural analysis
9. Being read to
10. Reading aloud

11. Reading silently
12. Creative writing
13. Reading for enjoyment
14. Enriching cultural background

Each teacher responded by marking "A great deal of time," "Some time," or "Little or no time."

Our examination of these reading activities, considered in light of our knowledge of curricular goals for elementary grades, led us to hypothesize three major categories for these items. *Readiness skills,* generally covered in kindergarten through second grade, included items 1 through 5. Items 6, 7, 8, 10, and 11 represented *reading skills* used in all elementary grades, though with different content. *Free reading for enjoyment, cultural enrichment, and creative writing,* items 9 and 12 to 14, are activities that also span all grades but that emphasize affect rather than skill development.

How might we confirm the appropriateness of this proposed structure? The approach we chose was to factor analyze the data from this subset of responses. You will note that we have not followed the common practice of factor analyzing the data for the entire questionnaire. Rather, we have selected specific questions for analysis where we had reason *a priori* to think that a simple structure might exist.

Factor analysis reduces a large number of items to a smaller number of factor scores, each of which represents an underlying pattern of related items. For instance, the "time on activities" correlation coefficients (Table 8-1) indicate the existence of three possible categories, shown by the triangles. To be sure, categories are not entirely independent of one another. The correlations within a group range from .20 to .64; the correlations outside the groups range from .03 to .34. *Sight vocabulary* is almost equally correlated with the items in categories I and II; and *reading silently* is correlated with the items in triangles II and III; nonetheless, the pattern is clear.

Factor analysis of the correlation coefficients produced three factors. Table 8-2 gives the item "loadings" for each factor score. A loading is the correlation between an item and a factor score (Mulaik, 1972). Overlapping items, like *sight vocabulary,* load strongly on two factors. All items vary in the strength of their relationship to the factor; the loadings for Factor II range from .40 for *reading aloud* to a high of .58 for *word meanings.*

We used factor analysis to confirm our *a priori* ideas about the natural clustering of items in the questionnaire. However, we decided not to use factor scores for the analyses presented in this chapter and the next. Factor scores have an abstract character, and require some experience for easy interpretation. Instead, we chose to use *average composite scores.* For instance, the six items which loaded strongly on Factor I were simply

Table 8-1
Correlation Coefficients for Time on Activities

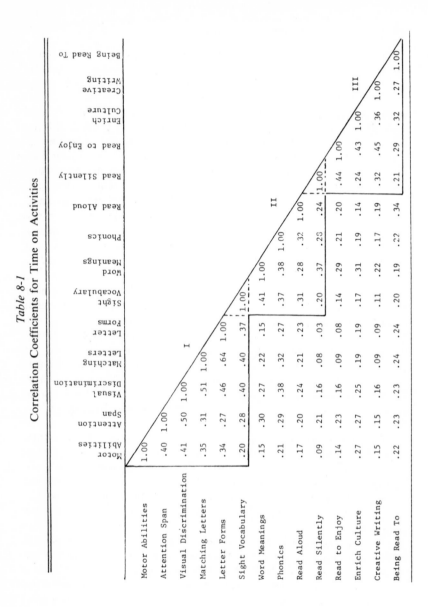

	Motor Abilities	Attention Span	Visual Discrimination	Matching Letters	Letter Forms	Sight Vocabulary	Word Meanings	Phonics	Read Aloud	Read Silently	Read to Enjoy	Enrich Culture	Creative Writing	Being Read To
Motor Abilities	1.00													
Attention Span	.40	1.00												
Visual Discrimination	.41	.50	1.00											
Matching Letters	.35	.31	.51	1.00										
Letter Forms	.34	.27	.46	.64	1.00									
Sight Vocabulary	.20	.28	.40	.40	.37	1.00								
Word Meanings	.15	.30	.27	.22	.15	.41	1.00							
Phonics	.21	.29	.38	.32	.27	.37	.38	1.00						
Read Aloud	.17	.20	.24	.21	.23	.31	.28	.32	1.00					
Read Silently	.09	.21	.16	.08	.03	.20	.37	.23	.24	1.00				
Read to Enjoy	.14	.23	.16	.09	.08	.14	.29	.21	.20	.44	1.00			
Enrich Culture	.27	.27	.25	.19	.19	.17	.31	.19	.14	.24	.43	1.00		
Creative Writing	.15	.15	.16	.09	.09	.11	.22	.17	.19	.32	.45	.36	1.00	
Being Read To	.22	.23	.23	.24	.24	.20	.19	.22	.34	.21	.29	.32	.27	1.00

I

II

III

Table 8-2
Loadings for Items Used to Form Three Factor Scores

Factor I		Factor II		Factor III	
Motor abilities	.64	Word Meanings	.58	Enriching Culture	.57
Attention span	.44	Phonics	.53	Read to enjoy	.71
Visual discrimination	.64	Reading aloud	.40	Creative writing	.58
Matching letters/words	.73	Reading silently	.43	Reading silently	.45
Letter forms	.71				
Sight vocabulary	.38	Sight vocabulary	.54	Being read to	.38

averaged to yield a teacher's composite score for that cluster. Composites lack the independence of true factor scores but are easier to understand.

Multiple-item questions were chosen for factor analysis according to two criteria. First, the question had to have a lot of subitems, five or more. For instance, the teachers were asked to rate their satisfaction, comparing their school with other schools in their district as to physical facilities, faculty, administration, the philosophy of education within the school, and student ability and attitudes. We hypothesized that, in this question, we might find consistent differences in feelings toward (a) student, (b) faculty and philosophy of education, and (c) administration and physical facilities. In essence, the first criterion was the existence of a complex question structure which seemed *a priori* to have a potentially simpler structure, making it a worthwhile venture to carry out (Korth, 1975).

The second criterion for selecting a multi-item question was that the resulting composite scores would be likely to have a conceptual relation with other scores in the survey. For instance, a teacher's attitudes toward his pupils and his beliefs about their capacity for learning might be expected to influence the learning activities he selects for the students.

This chapter describes the composite scores for teachers' *attitudes* toward staff and students, their judgments about major sources of *student problems,* their *goals* in reading for students, their instructional *practices,* and their feelings of *success* or failure in teaching. For each major category —Attitudes, Student Problems, Reading Goals, Reading Activities, and Success in Teaching—we also describe, where pertinent, the influence of several important variables: geographical region, urbanity, grade, experience, training and beliefs about the value of compensatory instruction.

Teacher Attitudes

Compensatory reading teachers in this study are, by definition, working with children who are having problems learning to read. The teaching task is often difficult, for whatever instruction was provided these children in prior years had failed to remedy their problems. "The gaps between the learning tasks and the 'readiness' of the children are a source of frustration to the teachers as well as the children" (Bloom, Davis, & Hess, 1965, p. 20). The teachers must continue the hope that their pupils can be helped, that with the right instruction their pupils can and will learn to read. If frustration leads to the belief that everything will stay pretty much the same—that able learners will learn and the less able will not, no matter what is done for them—then there is little hope for special compensatory programs.

Of course, the teacher's attitude toward pupils is also likely to reflect the general morale in the school. Do the teachers value one another? Do they believe that the administration is responsive to their needs?

The ETS questionnaire provides information about the teachers' feelings about the students, the faculty, the administration, and the general school philosophy. Through these responses we can get a tentative idea of teacher morale, and supposedly where the morale is high "student achievement is increased" (Harap, 1959). Unfortunately, there were no items concerning teachers' feelings about the community's attitudes and the degree of parental support. Such information might have been enlightening.

Four composite scores about teacher attitudes—one on the schools and the personnel and three on the students—will be examined in this section. First, the makeup and meaning of each score is described, and then its distribution. The scores are examined as a function of community and regional differences, experience, training, and grade.

School and Pupil Attitudes

Two multi-item questions fell under the heading of teacher attitudes. The first question was "Compared with other elementary schools in your district or community, how satisfied are you with respect to the following things about your school?" The "things" listed were (a) physical facilities, (b) faculty, (c) ability of student body, (d) attitudes of student body, (e) administration, and (f) overall philosophy of education. The choices for each ranged from "highly satisfied" to "highly dissatisfied."

Two factors were identified in this question (Tables 8-3 and 8-4). The first one, *Attitude toward Staff and School,* indicates that a teacher is likely to give similar ratings for the administration, the overall philosophy of education, and the other teachers in the school. The second factor, *Attitude toward Students,* shows that a teacher rated student ability about the same as student attitudes. The *physical facilities* item correlated

Table 8-3
Correlation Coefficients for the Six Items
in the *How Satisfied* Attitude Question

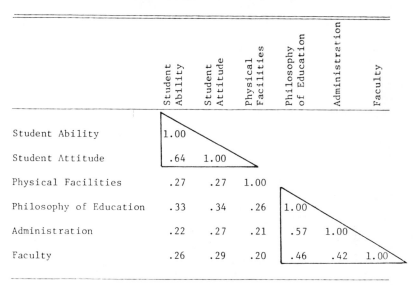

	Student Ability	Student Attitude	Physical Facilities	Philosophy of Education	Administration	Faculty
Student Ability	1.00					
Student Attitude	.64	1.00				
Physical Facilities	.27	.27	1.00			
Philosophy of Education	.33	.34	.26	1.00		
Administration	.22	.27	.21	.57	1.00	
Faculty	.26	.29	.20	.46	.42	1.00

Table 8-4
Factor Loadings, Means and Standard Deviations
for Items Used for Teacher Attitude Composite

Composite Items	Factor Loadings	m	s.d.	n
Attitudes toward Staff and School				
Administration	.73	1.69	.77	1817
Philosophy of Education	.75	1.77	.71	1816
Faculty	.54	1.50	.61	1825
Attitudes toward Students				
Ability	.79	2.00	.69	1817
Attitudes	.78	2.17	.78	1817

1 = Highly Satisfied to 4 = Highly Dissatisfied

weakly with all other items and was therefore not a member of either composite score.

Ideally, the two composites should be independent of each other, with little correlation between them. In fact, *Attitude toward Staff* correlated with *Attitude toward Students* at .39. This correlation is not negligible. Some people had a generally positive attitude, while others tended to be more negative. However, item correlations within a composite were stronger than the between-composite correlation, and the factor loadings also showed fairly strong relationships within each composite. The relatively smaller loading on *faculty* resulted because feelings toward faculty were uniformly positive; there was more variability in attitudes toward administration and school philosophy, and hence more opportunity for a correlation.

Next we want to consider certain features of the distributions of attitude composites. It may help to see how a teacher's responses were used to generate a composite, and so we have illustrated the procedure in Table 8-5 for one particular teacher.

Figure 8-1 shows the distribution of the attitude composites. The averages for *Attitude toward Staff and School* and *Attitude toward Students* indicate a high degree of satisfaction with the staff and school, and a generally moderate degree of satisfaction with the students. A noticeable minority of teachers were quite unhappy with their school assignment.

Academic Capabilities

The second attitude question asked about the academic capabilities of disadvantaged pupils (see also Chapter 4). The teacher rated 17 statements about pupils on a five-point scale from "strongly disagree" to "strongly agree." Factor analysis confirmed the existence of two composite scores (Table 8-6).

The first composite, *Learning Capacity of Disadvantaged*, combined two clusters which were inversely related to one another. The teacher who strongly believed that disadvantaged students can learn would disagree with the first four items and agree with the last two. If a teacher was equally strong in the belief that disadvantaged students can't learn, then he would produce the reverse pattern of scores.

The second composite score, *Disadvantaged Need Special Help*, is formed from seven items, which portray a situation where the disadvantaged student comes to school ill-prepared for learning, but with appropriate language training coupled with teacher encouragement can succeed in school. The item, *shorter attention span*, is common to both composites, and this communality partially accounts for the .28 correlation between the two scores. The distribution for the two composites, shown in Table 8-7, are quite similar; most teachers agree with the composite propositions.

Drum and Calfee

Table 8-5

A Hypothetical Teacher's Response to the
Original Question, and the Two Composite Scores
Based on these Responses

Code Value	Highly Satisfied (1)	Moderately Satisfied (2)	Moderately Dissatisfied (3)	Highly Dissatisfied (4)
Faculty	X	___	___	___
Philosophy	___	X	___	___
Administration	X	___	___	___
Facilities	___	X	___	___
Student Ability	___	X	___	___
Student Attitudes	___	___	X	___

Attitude toward Staff and School: (Faculty + Philosophy + Administration)/3 =

$$(1 + 2 + 1)/3 = 4/3 = 1.3$$

Attitude toward Students: (Student Ability + Student Attitude)/2 =

$$(2 + 3)/2 = 5/2 = 2.5$$

Note: Facilities is not part of either composite, so this score is not

shown above in the computations.

The teachers in the sample believed that the disadvantaged can learn but that they need special help in order to succeed. The most appropriate methods for helping might not require "complete verbal statements" and "improved self-concept"; these were the only choices available. What is important is that most of these teachers believed that something can be done and that low achieving students can be helped.

There were a few teachers (4 percent) who expressed moderate disagreement with the belief that low achievers can learn, and a significant number (30 percent) who were uncertain about learning capacity. One may question whether teacher expectations are a particularly potent factor in student learning (Braun, 1976), but it seems unlikely that the teacher who believes that students won't or can't learn will expend much effort trying different instructional techniques. If, as Durkin (1970) states, "no method, no matter how 'scientifically' worked out, . . . can take

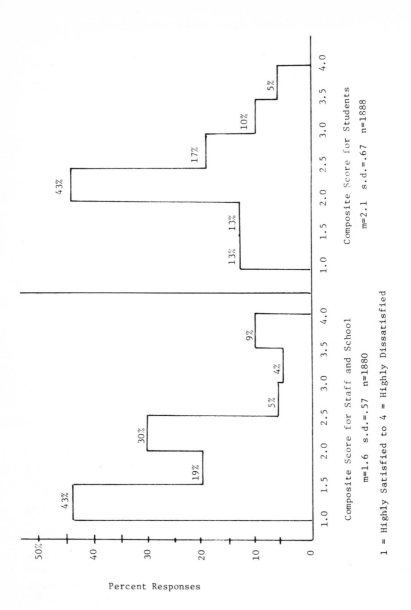

Figure 8-1. Attitudes toward staff and school, and toward students

Drum and Calfee

Table 8-6

Factor Loadings, Means and Standard Deviations
for Items Used in *Learning Capacity of Disadvantaged*
and *Disadvantaged Need Special Help* Composites

Composite Items	Factor Loadings	m	s.d.	n
Learning Capacity				
Always score lower	.68	2.43	.96	1814
Don't want to learn	.48	1.81	.78	1827
Never do as well	.62	2.18	.85	1827
Shorter attention span	.44	3.41	.98	1828
Can learn	-.61	3.45	1.00	1816
Wrong response is useful	-.25	3.96	.65	1823
Need Special Help				
More trouble reading	.49	3.81	.83	1827
Shorter attention span	.41	3.41	.98	1828
Fewer concepts	.51	3.78	.82	1815
Different linguistics	.52	4.04	.68	1827
Verbalization important	.54	3.94	.69	1823
Improve self-image	.41	4.53	.59	1828
Asking questions for complete answers helps	.39	3.56	.93	1818

1 = Strongly Disagree to 5= Strongly Agree

the place of a teacher who is both able and eager to succeed" (p. 8), then one wonders what will happen with teachers who accept failure before beginning.

Table 8-7
Percent of Teachers' Response on Disadvantaged Learning

	Learning Capacity	Need Special Help
Strongly agree	11	18
Moderately agree	53	62
Uncertain	30	17
Moderately disagree	4	1
Strongly disagree	0	0
Missing	2	2

(n = 1919)

Attitudes by Types of Community and Geographic Region

Teacher attitudes are quite favorable. However, there were detectable demographic trends (Table 8-8). Suburban teachers were most satisfied with both staff and students and urban teachers least satisfied; less than a tenth of a point separated the three groups. The geographical variations were slight, generally less than three-tenths of a point on a five-point scale for a single composite and should be considered only as trends.

Southern teachers had the most favorable attitudes toward staff but the least favorable attitude toward students. High morale is not so pervasive as to influence all aspects of one's job; it is possible to be well satisfied with the professional staff and yet not be terribly pleased with the students.

When one looks at *Capacity for Learning,* again the southern teachers felt that children had less capacity and needed more special help. In the West, on the other hand, teachers felt that the disadvantaged students had capacity for learning despite the fact that this region had the second lowest judgment on *Attitude toward Students.*

Attitudes by Teacher Training and Experience

In Table 8-9 are the composite means and standard deviations for teachers who had training in reading and those who had not, and for teachers with varied amounts of experience. Teachers who had taught more than six years tended to have a more favorable attitude toward

Table 8-8
Attitude Composites in Types of Community and in Geographic Regions

	Toward Staff			Toward Students			Capacity for Learning			Need Special Help		
	m	s.d.	n	m	s.d.	n	m	s.d.	n	m	s.d.	n
Type of Community												
Urban	2.10	.69	340	2.65	.88	341	2.41	.59	336	2.15	.48	341
Suburban	2.03	.70	687	2.56	.81	688	2.41	.52	688	2.13	.44	687
Rural	2.05	.74	594	2.63	.85	600	2.42	.55	592	2.11	.46	589
Geographical Region												
Northeast	2.07	.73	352	2.46	.86	352	2.36	.52	347	2.15	.43	353
North Central	2.10	.68	582	2.55	.74	586	2.43	.51	578	2.15	.45	581
South	1.99	.70	499	2.74	.89	503	2.49	.60	505	2.06	.48	496
West	2.10	.74	366	2.63	.86	365	2.31	.54	361	2.16	.45	362

The Toward Staff and Toward Students composites were rescaled on a five-point scale so that all four composites could be directly compared. 1 = Most Satisfied for the first two composites and Strongly Agree for the last two. 5 = Least Satisfied for the first two composites and Strongly Disagree for the last two.

Table 8-9
Attitude Composites by Teacher Experience and Training

	Toward Staff			Toward Students			Capacity for Learning			Need Special Help		
	m	s.d.	n	m	s.d.	n	m	s.d.	n	m	s.d.	n
Years Experience												
Less than 1	2.00	.71	136	2.69	.86	140	2.29	.49	138	2.13	.44	140
1 to 3	2.20	.73	200	2.80	.89	197	2.38	.50	196	2.13	.46	194
3 to 6	2.26	.70	326	2.63	.86	326	2.37	.49	321	2.12	.43	324
6 to 10	2.05	.74	317	2.47	.81	316	2.31	.56	313	2.14	.47	313
10 to 20	2.01	.64	481	2.61	.81	483	2.44	.56	484	2.13	.46	478
Over 20	1.90	.64	343	2.52	.81	348	2.58	.60	343	2.13	.46	347
Reading Training												
Yes	2.05	.71	1054	2.59	.85	1059	2.39	.56	1046	2.09	.44	1048
No	2.09	.70	742	2.64	.83	744	2.43	.54	740	2.18	.46	739

The Toward Staff and Toward Students composites were rescaled on a five-point scale so that all four composites could be directly compared. 1 = Most Satisfied for the first two composites and Strongly Agree for the last two. 5 = Least Satisfied for the first two composites and Strongly Disagree for the last two.

students and toward the staff. First year teachers were also more positive, but the excitement and idealism of the first year is replaced with a more critical view of both staff and students in teachers with one to three years' experience. The old saw of idealism meeting reality may be the source for this quick rise in discontent. The reversal in attitudes in Table 8-9 may be a result of the presumed inadequacies in preservice training. However, there is also the immediate joy of having a class of one's own without supervision from the professional school or from a master teacher and with the license of implementing one's own ideas. By the second year, the novice has learned that not all ideas work, that one encounters failure as well. Through the experience of teaching, one learns what ideas work and how to use failure to improve. Rather than being critical of others, the experienced teacher recognizes that all are working together on a difficult task.

There is no trend for experience on *Need for Special Help*, but teachers with ten years or more experience do have less confidence in the *Learning Capacity* of their disadvantaged students.

Teachers with special training in reading diagnosis and remediation had favorable attitudes toward staff and students, and they also believed the students had greater learning potential. Better preparation may indeed lessen the difficulty of the instructional task by providing teachers with tools to help their students. With an idea of the student's particular weakness and an instructional plan, a teacher is less likely to feel frustrated or to label the child as hopeless. In any event, the teachers with reading training were more satisfied with their students and with the staff than those without special training.

Attitudes and Belief in Compensatory Programs

A clear pattern emerges in the relation between attitudes and compensatory programs. A majority of the teachers (60 percent) believed that compensatory reading programs are definitely worthwhile and 51 percent believed that there is a sound basis for the extra cost encountered. However, the few who held the opposite view (2 percent) were also least satisfied with both students and staff. There was a consistent trend between judgment of *Learning Capacity* and the teachers' opinions on the value of compensatory programs. A strong belief in the program was coupled with a strong belief in capacity for learning, and vice versa. The *Need for Special Help* also followed this pattern of less perceived need for help and greater skepticism about the effectiveness of compensatory programs. A small number of teachers (3 percent) who felt that compensatory programs were probably worthless rather inexplicably believed in the value of special help. This group may have been commenting on the quality of the programs within their particular schools, rather than on compensatory programs generally.

Teacher Perceptions of Sources of Student Problems

In this section, we examine a question in which the teachers were asked to "estimate the percentage of pupils in your compensatory reading class who have persistent problems in each of the following areas: family instability, emotional problems, vision, hearing, speech, frequent illness, and mental retardation."

The correlations between these items turned up two factors (Table 8-10). Frequent illness appeared as a weak common denominator across all problems. Mental retardation was not perceived as a major source of problems and was not coupled with either composite to a significant degree. In fact, the negligible correlation with vision and hearing problems reflects a change in attitude over the years. Four decades ago it was common to assume that physically impaired people, particularly those with hearing losses, were also mentally retarded (Pinter, Eisenson, & Stanton, 1941).

The *Family and Emotion* composite shows that many teachers believed that a major source of the students' problems begins at home and leads to emotional maladjustment, which, in turn, makes it difficult for the child to learn in school. The teachers gave the opinion that about one-fifth of their compensatory students had some type of family and emotional problems. Emotional problems, of course, might range from children who can't sit still for more than fifteen minutes to children who are classroom isolates to the point of autism. Neither was it clear that emotional disorder was linked in the teacher's mind to the home environment. "While it is possible for teachers and school administrators to blame the home and the parents for the difficulties these children have in learning, this placement of blame does little good for the child or teacher who must deal with him" (Bloom et al., 1965, p. 22).

Vision and Hearing is the second composite. Teachers judged that approximately five percent of the compensatory students had a vision or hearing problem. Teachers can alter instruction and request special materials for certain mild impairments, but most do not have the training or equipment for major problems. It seems likely that the five percent of the compensatory students were only mildly handicapped. The new federal and state laws on education of the handicapped in regular classrooms are likely to change this situation, especially in compensatory classrooms. We can only hope that the increased demand on the teachers is accompanied by adequate assistance. In 1971-72, it was not such a great problem.

Problems by Type of Community and Geographic Region

Family and emotional problems increase as one moves away from the Northeast, and toward the South and West (Table 8-11). Interestingly, this pattern parallels the dissatisfaction with students in the South and

Table 8-10
Factor Loadings, Mean Percent, and Standard Deviations
for Items Used for Student Problems Composites

	Factor Loadings	m	s.d.	n
Family and Emotion				
Emotional Problems	.80	17	19	1803
Family Problems	.60	21	22	1742
Vision and Hearing				
Vision	.56	7	12	1787
Hearing	.61	3	6	1731

Table 8-11
Mean Percent of Students for Problem Composites
in Types of Community and Geographic Regions

	Family and Emotion			Vision and Hearing		
	m	s.d.	n	m	s.d.	n
Types of Community						
Urban	21	18	300	5	7	298
Suburban	19	19	630	6	9	622
Rural	18	18	523	5	6	536
Geographic Region						
Northeast	17	19	321	6	9	319
North Central	17	18	515	5	7	521
South	19	19	424	5	7	441
West	22	19	344	5	9	333

West (Table 8-8). Both population mobility and the increased divorce rate in western states seem likely to contribute to family instability. Moving from one location to another upsets the child's schooling and cuts him off from his friends. When "moving-on" is a pattern in the child's life, and when parental roles change, the resulting insecurity can interfere with learning in school.

Student Problems and Teacher Experience and Training

The influence of experience and training on the problem composites was slight, and not worth reporting in detail. A few trends will be mentioned. Teachers with twenty or more years' experience showed a tendency to believe that emotional maladjustment was an insignificant student problem. Highly experienced teachers (twenty years or more) and brand new teachers rated *Vision and Hearing* as less of a problem than those with between one to twenty years' experience. Teachers with training in diagnosis were more likely to believe that their students had family and emotional problems than were teachers without training.

Overall, emotional and family problems were seen as important contributors to the below-average performance of compensatory readers. Approximately a fifth of these children were believed to have such problems. What was being done to help them? In response to "What other professionals (counselors and psychologists) are available to you in your teaching of compensatory reading?" only 10 percent of the 1833 teachers said they had such help frequently. Forty-six percent said professional assistance was rare or not available, while 13 percent did not answer this question. If this composite identifies a major source of student problems, then it appears that little was being done to help the students or their teachers.

Goals for Reading

The next question looks at what the teachers intend to accomplish in order to help these children learn to read. What goals are seen as most useful for elementary students in compensatory reading programs?

Teachers were asked to rate the importance of 24 classroom activities as goals for their current teaching of compensatory reading. A goal is usually considered an intended outcome; what one would like to happen as a result of planned effort. This list combined both goals and activities. For instance, matching letters or words is probably not a goal, but instead a means of learning letter forms and developing a slight vocabulary, which are more proper goals.

The 24 items include considerable variety: pure affect ("improving self-image"), measurement of reading progress ("reading aloud"), and

Drum and Calfee

writing exercises ("practicing punctuation and paragraph skills"). The list also contains some surprising choices, considering the grade levels in the survey. For instance, it seems unlikely that many second, fourth, and sixth grade teachers would have as a goal "improving motor abilities related to reading."

Three composites, *Readiness Goals, Skill Goals,* and *Affect Goals,* were identified in this question (Table 8-12). The patterns of factor loadings indicate that certain individual goals were especially important in the makeup of a particular composite, while other goals were subsidiary. Under the *Readiness* composite, auditory discrimination, matching letters and words, and learning better forms contributed more strongly than did reading aloud and improving listening skills. This differential loading is important to remember when interpreting a composite score. The *Readiness Goal* composite included fairly consistent responses for matching letters, letter forms, and auditory discrimination, but responses to reading aloud, phonics, listening, etc., are more variable. Several items loaded on two of the composites, such as phonics at .35 on *Readiness Goals* and on *Skill Goals* at .28. The double loading weakens the independence of the scores, as indicated by the correlations, particularly the .69 between *Skill Goals* and *Affect Goals* (Table 8-13).

Goals by Grade

Because of the nature of the items, it is enlightening to examine the goals by grade (Figure 8-2). *Readiness Goals* should be and were much more important in second grade than in fourth or sixth grades. What is surprising is the importance of these goals as a secondary goal for the upper grades. Of course, this may simply reflect the teacher's unwillingness to mark "Not a Goal."

There was substantial tendency, except among second grade teachers, for *Skill Goals* to assume major importance, with context clues, comprehension, and punctuation and paragraph skills (a slightly peculiar choice) the most important items. Silent reading was seen as less important, perhaps because it was a less observable goal than "increase in reading rate."

The *Affect Goals* were pervasive across the three grades. About 70 percent of the teachers believed affect to be a major goal, and most of the rest listed it as a secondary goal. Only the teachers of the ungraded classes tended to see affect as a less important goal than the other teachers.

The responses for the three composite goals were fairly constant over community and geographic regions, and will not be presented in detail. Teacher training, experience, and beliefs about the value of compensatory program also had little effect on the goal composites, and will not be discussed here.

Table 8-12
Factor Loadings for Items in Goal Composites

Readiness Goals		Skill Goals		Affect Goals	
Motor Ability	.55	Word Meanings	.43	Verbal Communication	.50
Attention Span	.48	Context Clues	.58	Creative Writing	.42
Auditory Discrimination	.74	Syllabification	.45	Enrich Culture	.50
Matching Letters & Words	.73	Comprehension	.57	Improve Self-Image	.56
Learning Letter Forms	.72	Reading Rate	.43	Improve Reading Attitudes	.53
Reading Aloud	.27	Reading Silently	.39	Read to Enjoy	.42
Sight Vocabulary	.36	Phonics	.28		
Phonics	.35			Listening	.29
Listening	.33				

Punctuation	.52	Punctuation	.27
Study Skills	.42	Study Skills	.32
Library Skills	.37	Library Skills	.42

Table 8-13
Correlations for the Goal Composites

	Readiness	Skill	Affect
Readiness	1.00		
Skill	.34	1.00	
Affect	.39	.69	1.00

Goals and Attitudes

We are surprised to discover that goals were not related to attitudes or to perceived problems. The correlations of the two composite problem scores with the three goal scores range from —.05 to .08. The teachers' attitudes towards students, beliefs about learning capacity, and need for special help do not predict the goals either; the correlations range from —.09 to .02.

Reading Activities

The questionnaire included several questions pertaining to instructional practices in the teacher's classroom. Some of these questions have been covered earlier. The use and creation of different materials for instruction have been described in Chapter 7, the instructional practices in Chapter 6, and so forth.

We decided to focus our analysis on the information provided by question 33: "How much time does a typical pupil in your compensatory reading class spend in each of the following types of activity?" The reason for this selection was that the 14 items listed were exactly the same as 14 of the 24 listed under goals. We would expect a strong relationship between activities and goals, if the teachers were consistent in putting intention into practice. Also, the time a teacher chooses to spend on a specific task is a good indication of what that teacher believes to be most important in teaching reading. In fact, it may be a more specific and therefore more enlightening indication than a general statement about reading instruction. If a teacher claims to use a language experience approach, but then spends a great deal of time on visual discrimination, matching letters and words, and learning letter forms, this is certainly a different version of language experience than Stauffer (1970) described.

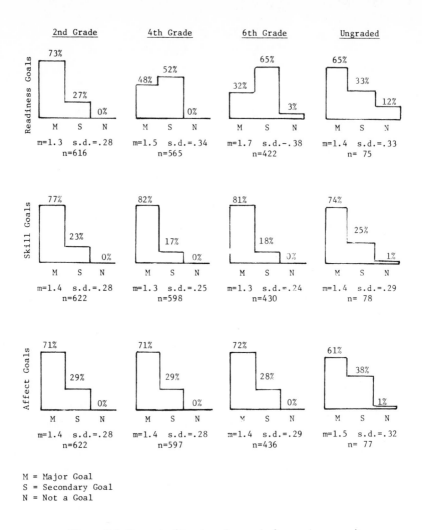

M = Major Goal
S = Secondary Goal
N = Not a Goal

Figure 8-2. Percent of teachers by grade for goal composites

The amount of time allotted to specific instructional activities could have been an excellent measure for discerning what the teachers actually believed was important for their students. Unfortunately, the response choices for question 33 were somewhat vague: 1) a great deal of time, 2) some time, and 3) little time or none. These responses do not pin down specific allocation of time per week from these choices, but only point to the general importance of the activity.

Three composite scores, *Readiness Activities, Skill Activities,* and *Affect Activities,* were confirmed by the factor analysis (Table 8-14). The items for each composite are similar to those of the goal composites, and the pattern of factor loadings also resemble one another. Sight vocabulary now loads on both *Readiness* and *Skills,* while phonics is now located in Skills alone. Reading silently is now part of the Affect composite as well as Skills. This sharing of items is one reason for the moderately strong correlations among the composites (Table 8-15).

The original 14 items necessarily covered a restricted set of reading activities. The teachers were not able to indicate how they spent time on context cues, comprehension activities such as recognizing gist, comparisons between passages, locating major ideas, etc. The list emphasized readiness activities, which is a bit unusual for a study spanning the elementary grades. The assumption may have been that students reading below grade level must repeat the activities of kindergarteners and first graders, since they failed to profit from these activities the first time around. This assumption can be questioned. More to the point, the limitations on the range of activities restrict the picture we can gain about the nature of elementary reading instruction in compensatory programs. Much more might be happening in the classrooms than this question reveals.

Grade and Activity Composites

The composites show a tendency for teachers to spend most time on *Skill Activities,* then *Affect,* and least on *Readiness* (Figure 8-3). The actual distributions vary with grade, with the ungraded classes quite unlike the others. Less time is spent on all three sets of activities, particularly on *Readiness,* as one progresses from second grade through sixth. The ungraded teachers reverse this pattern, as might be predicted from their heavy emphasis on prereading goals (Figure 8-2). The upper end of the average range for the ungraded students is 11.10 years; the older students would have been attending reading classes for five to six years. Readiness drills for these elementary children must be like death and taxes for adults—always with them.

While the composites show a decline in reading from second through sixth grade, a slightly different picture is suggested from the responses to specific items. In Table 8-16, the average ratings for items decrease from second to sixth grade for all activities except *Word Meanings* and *Reading Silently.* As the children get older, more time probably is spent on content materials, such as mathematics, science, and social studies; now reading is used for learning rather than something to be learned. Questions on teaching techniques for different materials might have clarified this deemphasis on reading instruction and the greater role of reading in the content areas. Both fourth and sixth grade teachers spend time teaching the technical vocabulary of mathematics and science, in explaining graphs

Table 8-14

Factor Loadings for Time on Activities Composites

Readiness Activities		Skill Activities		Affect Activities	
Motor Abilities	.52	Word Meanings	.58	Enriching Culture	.57
Attention Span	.44	Phonics	.53	Read to Enjoy	.71
Visual Discrimination	.64	Reading Aloud	.40	Creative Writing	.58
Matching Letters & Words	.73	Reading Silently	.43	Reading Silently	.45
Letter Forms	.71	Sight Vocabulary	.54		
Sight Vocabulary	.38			Being Read to	.38

1 = A Great Deal of Time to 3 = Little to No Time

Table 8-15
Correlation between Activity Composites

Activities	Readiness	Skills	Affect
Readiness	1.00		
Skills	.50	1.00	
Affect	.21	.55	1.00

and maps, in illustrating comparisons within texts. Many teachers may have felt that this instruction should not be considered compensatory reading and so did not include it.

Activity and Goal Composites

The goal and the activity composites are strongly related (Table 8-17). This makes sense when one considers the similarities between the item sets. Generally speaking, the correlation is highest along the diagonal in Table 8-17, which also makes sense and supports the adequacy of the composite scores as summaries. Teachers are consistent. We will examine this consistency in more detail in the next chapter.

Attitudes and Activities

The correlations between attitudes and activities are again quite weak, from —.09 to .11, as was the case between attitudes and goals. Slight trends do occur for the *Readiness Activities.* Emphasis on these activities indicates a stronger position on *Family and Emotion* as the source of problems, less belief in the disadvantaged's *Capacity for Learning,* and greater emphasis on *Need for Special Help.* Readiness also has the highest correlation with satisfaction with staff.

Activities, Training, Experience, and Demographic Factors

The activity composites will be used as primary criterion measures in the analysis in the next chapter, so we will defer further discussion of these scores until later. Only *Readiness Activities* fluctuate to any extent as a function of demographic variables. Southern teachers and teachers with training or with twenty or more years of experience spent more time on *Readiness* than they did on *Affect.*

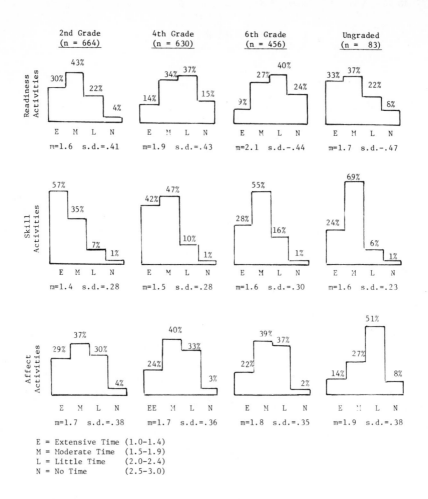

Figure 8-3. Percent of teachers by grade for time on activities

Feelings of Success

The teachers questioned in this survey provided reading instruction for the less able students who had not learned to read at an adequate level in regular instructional programs. Most of the teachers felt that compensatory or "catch-up" programs were definitely worthwhile, but how successful did they feel about their particular efforts? Question 45 asked "How successful would you consider your compensatory teaching to be with respect to the following criteria?" The data for two composites, *Self-Concept Success* and *Reading Achievement Success,* are shown in

Table 8-16
Means and Standard Deviations by Grade for Time on Activities

Activity	2nd Grade (n=664)		4th Grade (n=630)		6th Grade (n=456)		Ungraded (n=83)	
	m	s.d.	m	s.d.	m	s.d.	m	s.d.
Motor Abilities	1.97	.69	2.19	.70	2.29	.69	2.00	.70
Attention Span	1.65	.61	1.72	.61	1.81	.61	1.60	.66
Visual Discrimination	1.48	.62	1.74	.67	1.89	.68	1.47	.63
Matching Letters & Words	1.75	.69	2.09	.70	2.26	.71	1.89	.77
Letter Forms	1.77	.73	2.26	.70	2.50	.66	1.90	.83
Sight Vocabulary	1.37	.57	1.51	.72	1.64	.66	1.42	.57
Word Meanings*	1.38	.54	1.28	.48	1.27	.47	1.34	.52
Phonics	1.17	.44	1.37	.56	1.58	.62	1.25	.49
Reading Aloud	1.40	.54	1.63	.57	1.79	.64	1.72	.69
Reading Silently*	1.42	.59	1.39	.55	1.32	.50	1.66	.61
Being Read to	1.79	.58	1.96	.57	2.12	.60	2.10	.56
Read to Enjoy	1.61	.59	1.61	.61	1.57	.58	1.75	.64
Creative Writing	1.92	.65	1.95	.62	1.96	.67	2.17	.60
Enrich Culture	1.98	.64	1.99	.62	1.97	.62	2.06	.67

1 = A Great Deal of Time to 3 = Little to No Time

*Items that increase over grades in time allotment

Table 8-17
Correlations among Goal and Activity Composites

Activities	Goals		
	Readiness	Skill	Affect
Readiness	.64	.10	.18
Skill	.36	.22	.18
Affect	.11	.25	.41

Table 8-18. "Remediating cultural deprivation" loaded weakly on both factors and was not included in either composite.

The distribution of responses for the two composite scores (Figure 8-4) indicated that at all grades the teachers felt quite successful in raising *Self-Concept*. They reported that they improved student self-image and student attitudes toward reading. They were somewhat less successful in improving reading achievement, either readiness or measured skills. On both of these scores, success rather than failure was the general trend. These teachers believed that they were meeting their goals and that their instructional programs helped their students.

Success by Grade

There is little difference by grade for feelings of success in improving the students' self-concept, though sixth-grade teachers are inclined to feel somewhat less successful than teachers in earlier grades. Since over 50 percent of the sixth-grade teachers have students who have gone through at least two years of compensatory reading, it is reasonable for them to be less sure of success (Figure 8-5). It is surprising that ungraded teachers feel so successful in their efforts; 99 percent of them believe themselves

Table 8-18

Factor Loadings, Means and Standard Deviations
for Items Used for Teacher Feeling of Success Composites
and Percent of Teachers Selecting Each Item

Composite Items	Factor Loadings	Item Values		
		m	s.d.	n
Self-Concept Success				
Self-Image	.84	1.63	.30	1798
Attitudes toward Reading	.63	1.61	.56	1800
Reading Achievement Success				
Reading Achievement	.61	1.84	.56	1773
Prereading Skills	.55	1.89	.49	1627

1 = Very Successful to 4 = Very Unsuccessful

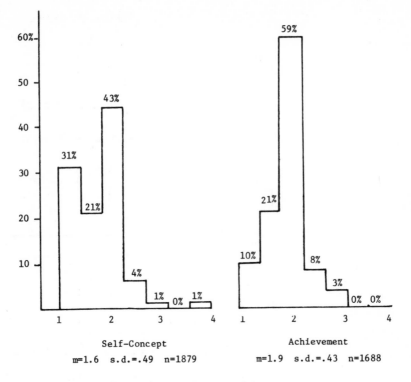

Self-Concept
m=1.6 s.d.=.49 n=1879

Achievement
m=1.9 s.d.=.43 n=1688

1 = Very Successful to 4= Very Unsuccessful

Figure 8-4. Feelings of success

moderately to quite successful in improving self-image and attitudes toward reading. These teachers held *Affect Goals* less strongly and spent the least amount of time on *Affect Activities,* and yet believed they had most success in this area.

In all grades, the teachers were less inclined to feel totally successful in improving reading achievement. Ungraded and second-grade teachers were equally optimistic, but both fourth- and particularly sixth-grade teachers felt that their students could have made more reading improvement.

Success and Goals and Activities

The relationships between reading goals and the teacher's feeling of success are fairly weak. All the correlations are positive, with activities

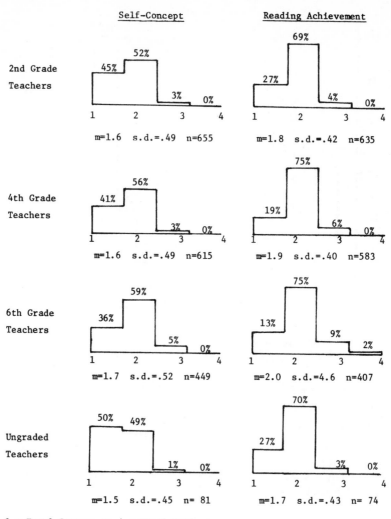

Self-Concept   Reading Achievement

2nd Grade Teachers

m=1.6   s.d.=.49   n=655   m=1.8   s.d.=.42   n=635

4th Grade Teachers

m=1.6   s.d.=.49   n=615   m=1.9   s.d.=.40   n=583

6th Grade Teachers

m=1.7   s.d.=.52   n=449   m=2.0   s.d.=4.6   n=407

Ungraded Teachers

m=1.5   s.d.=.45   n= 81   m=1.7   s.d.=.43   n= 74

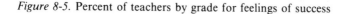

1 = Total Success to 4 = Total Failure

Figure 8-5. Percent of teachers by grade for feelings of success

showing stronger relationships with success than goals (Table 8-19). This pattern supports the argument that the actual time on activities is more important to success than statements about goals. It is important to recall that we are dealing with teacher perceptions throughout, and not with performance outcomes.

Table 8-19
Correlations among Success Composite
and Goal and Activity Composites

	Self-Concept Success	Reading Achievement Success
Readiness Goals	.11	.07
Skill Goals	.07	.08
Affect Goals	.15	.08
Readiness Activities	.16	.11
Skill Activities	.12	.17
Affect Activities	.20	.11

Success and Attitudes

All of these relationships are quite small, from —.08 to .20, with most of them fluctuating around zero, so trends should be viewed with caution. If a teacher feels that he has improved *Self-Concept*, then he also has a favorable view of the staff and an even more favorable view of the students, believing they have the capacity to learn. They do need special help, for they have family and emotional problems and, to a lesser extent, some physical impairments.

The same patterns show up for *Reading Achievement Success*, except that the teachers believe that family and emotional problems are negatively correlated with success, and no relationship is found with physical problems.

Success by Experience and Training

New teachers, those with less than six years' experience, feel least successful in their efforts to improve reading. There is a definite trend to feel more successful in this area if one has taught from six to twenty years. The most experienced teachers (over 20 years) are inclined to be more dubious about their success in improving measured reading achievement.

Though improving self-concept is generally an area of greater perceived success, teachers of three to six years' experience have doubts. All other teachers appear to be quite confident that their instruction has helped compensatory students improve their self-image and their attitudes toward reading.

Teachers who have had special training in reading are more optimistic about their success in improving reading skills and in raising the students' self-concept than teachers who have not had extra training. This may result from more accurate assessment of specific gains in reading. Improved reading rate or knowledge of short/long vowel distinctions are more recognizable outcomes than global changes in "reading."

Success by Types of Community and Geographical Region

Urban teachers are less sure that they have improved reading skills than suburban and rural teachers, but all three groups are equally certain that their students have a better self-image and a more favorable attitude toward reading as the result of instruction.

The only regional difference is that teachers in the Northeast feel somewhat more successful on both composites, and Western teachers believe they have raised reading skills more than Southern and North Central teachers.

These differences are small, and the major result over all groups—trained or untrained, experienced or inexperienced, urban or rural—is that there is a high level of perceived success in improving self-concept and a more moderate level of success in improving reading achievement. The teachers sampled were surprisingly homogeneous in their feelings of success. There were some differential trends, but the fluctuations were mainly between extreme satisfaction and moderate satisfaction.

In summary, these teachers were positive. They respected themselves and their professional staffs. Though they felt that most of their compensatory students did not have the appropriate linguistic or conceptual background for school learning, the teachers believed that the students had the desire and capacity to learn. The teachers' goals for compensatory reading were reflected in how they spent time on specific reading activities. Skills and attitudes were both seen as important, and opportunities were provided for the children to develop reading skills and favorable attitudes. The teachers' perceived success in reaching these goals must be seen in the context of the children who had been assigned to compensatory programs because of their inadequate performance. Any gain may appear as a mark of the teachers' success, even though the gain may be small and insufficient for functional literacy.

We were troubled by two findings in this section of the survey. The teachers cited the family and emotional problems as major sources for the students' poor performance. Whether or not this is an accurate reaction, schools cannot do much to change the home environment. The curriculum, the classroom activities, and the teacher's instructional program are under control of the school, and the task is to fit this program to the special needs of the children. In the ideal case, home and school work together for the student's benefit. Much is said today about accountability, but teachers have little practical guidance about how to fulfill their roles when the home, for social and economic reasons, cannot provide support for the student's educational growth. Clarification of this issue is sorely needed. Certainly the school cannot solve all the student's needs; neither is it enough to simply point to the home as the source of the difficulty.

The other area of concern is the finding that teachers spent less time on reading in the upper elementary grades. This may be an artifact of the questionnaire limitations, as noted earlier. If the student cannot read well enough for his school work, and if yearly gains are marginal, then more rather than less time should be allocated to help older students catch up with their peers and with the demands of the curriculum.

Chapter 9

Teaching Goals and Teaching Time in Compensatory Reading Programs

Robert C. Calfee
Stanford University
Priscilla A. Drum
University of California at Santa Barbara

We discussed in the previous chapter a method for summarizing the information from selected items on the questionnaire by means of *composite scores*. We indicated how these composites were constructed and presented descriptive statistics for the measures. In this chapter, we will look at how the Goal and Time composites are influenced by features of the teacher's background and attitude, by the income level of the community in which the school is located, and by characteristics of the particular class being taught. We will also examine the relations between the Goal and Time composites.

To refresh your memory, here are the Goal and Time composites from the analysis in Chapter 8:

Goals

How important are each of these activities as goals
of your compensatory reading program?

Readiness Activities	*Skill Activities*	*Free Reading*
Motor abilities	Vocabulary	Paragraph
Attention	Phonics	Library study skills
Auditory skills	Context clues	Verbal communication
Matching	Syllables	Creative writing
Learning letters	Punctuation	Reading enjoyment
Sight words	Comprehension	Cultural enrichment
Phonics	Improved rate	Self image
Listening	Silent reading	Better attitude
Reading aloud	Library study skills	

Time

How much time does your class spend on each of these activities
as part of the compensatory reading program?

Reading Activities	*Skill Activities*
Motor abilities	Sight words
Attention	Vocabulary
Visual discrimination	Phonics
Matching	Being read to
Learning letters	Reading aloud
Sight words	Reading silently

The third Time composite, Affect Activities, was based on few items and was unreliable, so we will not attempt further analysis here.

If you compare the items in the Goals and Time composites, you will see that the match between the two is not perfect. There are different numbers of items, and there are slightly different assignments of items to composites. It is unfortunate that the questionnaire was not designed to achieve a closer parallel between goals and time because this would have strengthened the analysis we are about to describe. The chief aim of our analysis is to examine individual differences in teachers' goals, to gain an understanding of how background variables influenced these goals, and to explore the effects of goals and other background variables on teachers' judgments of how they spent time in reading. Despite the mismatches, the analysis turns out to be quite enlightening.

Summary of Composite Measures by Average and Contrast Scores

We will organize our analysis around the following questions:

1. In general, over all areas of the curriculum, how important are reading goals to the teacher of compensatory reading?
2. What is the relative importance of readiness as contrasted with skills?
3. What is the relative importance of skills as contrasted with free reading?
4. In general, over all areas of the curriculum, how much time does the teacher assign to reading?
5. What is the relative commitment of time to readiness as opposed to skills?

Average scores. If you study this list of questions, you will see that two of the questions (1 and 4) ask about the teacher's average rating over all the composite measures for Goals and for Time, respectively. The measures for answering these two questions are quite straightforward— we calculate the average of a teacher's goal composites to answer question

1 and the average of the time composites to answer question 4. We will refer to these as *Goal Average* and *Time Average*, respectively.

Contrast scores. Answering the other three questions requires a different approach. Each of these questions focuses on a comparison of the relative importance of two composites. For instance, a teacher may stress readiness more than skills, quite apart from the overall level of importance he assigns to reading. To measure this comparison, we calculate the *weighted difference* between the two composites. In the statistical literature, such a difference is known as a *contrast* score. Table 9-1 illustrates how two typical teachers' composite scores are used to calculate average and contrast scores for answering each of the five questions listed above. This table should give you an idea of how the measures operate.

This approach may seem unconventional, but in fact, you may have relied on it if you have carried out individual intelligence testing. A test like the WISC (Wechsler, 1949) has two useful summary measures—the student's *overall IQ score* (the average over all items in the test), and the *difference between Verbal and Performance IQ* (the contrast between the two scales). Both measures contain useful information, in the opinion of many clinicians (Searls, 1975). Finding that a student has a high IQ is useful information; learning that his Performance IQ is considerably higher than his Verbal IQ is also useful information in its own right. Our use of average and contrast scores is intended to serve a similar purpose in understanding teachers' judgments about their goals in relation to their allocation of time.

Relations between scores. Average and contrast scores were calculated for each teacher who was responsible for a compensatory reading program. Figure 9-1 shows the distribution of these scores, and correlations are presented in Table 9-2. The reliability for each score is also presented in the table. The averages are quite reliable, especially considering the diversity of the items. The reliability of the contrast scores is lower, but this is to be expected since the items were not selected to maximize specific contrasts (Calfee, Drum, & Arnold, 1978).

As you can see from the figure, most teachers rated reading Goals somewhere between "major" and "secondary," on the average. The Time Average was lower, generally closer to the middle category, "some," than to "a great deal." The rating scales for Goals and for Time are not equivalent, but the evidence suggests that the teachers assigned reading a higher place in their intentions than in their practices.

The contrast scores provide additional detail on these ratings. Readiness was a relatively less important goal than Skill development for most teachers. The variability was considerable, to be sure, and many teachers showed no preference between these two goal areas, or actually held higher goals within the Readiness category. There was no preference for free reading over the two skills categories combined—the average score for this contrast was zero.

Table 9-1

Illustration of How Average and Contrast Scores are Derived from Composite Scores

GOAL
1 = Major
2 = Secondary
3 = Little or No Importance

| | Composites | | | Average | Contrast: Readi (+) vs Skill (-) | Contrast: Readi/Skills (+) vs Free (-) |
	Readi-ness	Skills	Free Reading			
Teacher A	2.00	2.50	2.75	2.42	-.50	-.50
Teacher B	1.50	1.50	2.75	1.92	.00	-1.25

TIME
1 = A Great Deal
2 = Some
3 = Little or None

| | Composites | | Average | Contrast: Readi (+) vs Skill (-) |
	Readi-ness	Skills		
Teacher A	1.50	2.00	1.75	-.50
Teacher B	1.75	1.25	1.50	.50

Profile Interpretation:

Teacher A assigns reading a low priority on the average between "Secondary" and "Little or No Importance." An average of "3" is the lowest possible, and he is not far from there. He judges Readiness to be a bit more important than Skills. The greatest difference in this direction would occur if a teacher always judged Readiness items as "Major" and Skills as "Unimportant." Then the contrast would be (Readiness = 1) – (Skills = 3) or –2. Teacher A has a slight tendency in this direction, for both Goals and Time. He also favors Reading Skills to Free Reading, as shown by the negative contrast score for Skills vs Free Reading under Goals.

Teacher B has a very different profile from Teacher A and shows an inconsitency between the Goals and Time Contrasts for Readiness vs Skills. He says that his goals for Readiness and Skills are equally important, but he spends less time on Readiness.

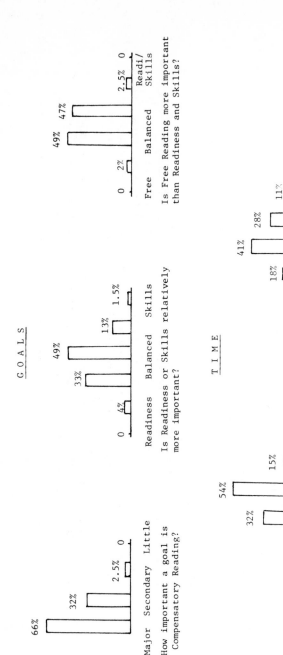

G O A L S

How important a goal is Compensatory Reading?

Is Readiness or Skills relatively more important?

Is Free Reading more important than Readiness and Skills?

T I M E

How much reading time on the average?

More time on Readiness or on Skills?

Figure 9-1. Distribution of Average and Contrast scores for Goals and Time composites

Calfee and Drum

Table 9-2
Descriptive Statistics and Correlations for Time and Goal Averages and Contrast Scores
(N = 1668)

Measure	Range	GOAL Avg	GOAL Readi/ Skills	GOAL Skills /Free	TIME Avg	TIME Readi/ Skills	Mean	Standard Deviation	Reliability
GOAL									
Average	1 = Major, 3 = Unimportant	-	**45**	04	30	31	1.4	.30	.80
Readiness vs Skills	-2 = Readiness, +2 = Skills		-	**48**	28	18	.1	.53	.55
Skills vs Free Reading	-2 = Skills, +2 = Free			-	15	06	.0	.40	.25
TIME									
Average	1 = Much, 3 = Little				-	**44**	1.7	.33	.74
Readiness vs Skills	-2 = Readiness, +2 = Skills					-	.4	.51	.37

Note: Decimals omitted in correlations; bold face correlations significant at p < .01

Teaching Goals

The correlations in the table show that the five measures do not have a uniformly close relation. Only three of the correlations account for more than ten percent of the variance between a pair of measures. One of these is the correlation between Goal Average and the Contrast of Readiness versus Skills. Teachers who assign a high rating to reading goals on the average also tend to place more weight on the teaching of skills as opposed to readiness. A similar description holds for the correlation between the Time Average and the Time Contrast for Readiness versus Skills. The third correlation of any size is between the two Goal Contrast scores. What happens here is that teachers who favor skills over readiness also prefer free reading to skill development as goals for their classes. Teachers who place reading generally high on their instructional goals place special emphasis on the value of reading for enjoyment and self-enhancement.

Prediction of Goals and Time

Regression with Multiple Predictors

The approach we will use to untangle the relationships in the Goals and Time scores is known as multiple regression (Kerlinger & Pedhazur, 1973). In an ordinary regression analysis, the direct relation between two variables is measured—for instance, you might find a strong tendency for height to increase steadily with age, at least up through the age of eighteen. In a *multiple* regression, several predictor variables are brought together to form the predictive equation. The relation between height and age is not perfect—what other variables might influence height? One possibility is the child's nutritional history. In the multiple regression procedure, after age has been used to predict height as closely as possible, the secondary variable of nutritional history is given a chance to predict the remaining variability.

The multiple regression procedure has an advantage over simple correlation in that it describes the overall structure of the relations in a network of variables. The measures we are examining are all correlated to some extent. The multiple regression describes the strength of relation between the dependent measure and each of the predictors, taking into account the total structure of correlations.

The F-ratio. The contribution of each predictor variable in a multiple regression is measured by two indices. The F-ratio, an index of statistical significance, is the ratio between the predicted variability from a particular source and the residual or unpredicted variability. For instance, if the F-ratio for the effect of age on height were equal to 216.3, this would mean that the variation in height predicted by age was more than two hundred times as large as the residual variability. This comparison tells us whether we have learned anything from the predictor. If a predictor variable has only a random influence on the dependent measure, we would expect the F-ratio to be about equal to 1.0. This would happen if the "predicted" variability were about the same as the error of measurement. If the F-ratio is many times larger than 1.0, this means that the likelihood is low that there is only a chance relation between the predictor variable and the depending measure.

The beta weight. The second index of the importance of a predictor is the "beta weight." Following our earlier example, the multiple regression procedure would produce the prediction equation:

$$\text{Height} = (\text{Beta}_{age} * \text{Age}) + (\text{Beta}_{nutrition} * \text{Nutrition}) + \text{Error}$$

That is, the height of a person is described by the equation as a function of his age multiplied by a beta index for age, plus his nutritional history multiplied by beta index for nutrition. If the beta weight for a given predictor variable is close to zero, then that predictor does not influence the predicted height very strongly. Weights greater than about .2 generally have a practical value for prediction in situations of the sort we will be considering.

Applying the multiple regression approach. We have now described how we intend to analyze measures for each of the five questions raised at the beginning of the chapter. We will first calculate the multiple regression to learn how the Goal Averages and Contrasts are related to indices of the teacher's background, the community, and the class. Next we will analyze the Time scores. We feel that these are important measures of what the teacher does in the classroom. The Goal scores reflect intention—the Time scores point to action. We realize that the Time scores are only judgments and are not necessarily accurate descriptions of events in the classroom. However, teachers are reasonably aware of what they do, and there was little reason in this survey for teachers to exaggerate. We will once more use the teacher's background, the community, and the class characteristics to predict Time scores. We will also use the teacher's Goal scores to predict Time scores, in order to determine the strength of the relation between what the teacher says he intends to do and what he says he tries to do.

Expected results. What should we expect from this analysis? The overall accuracy of a multiple regression equation is measured by a coefficient, R. Like the regular correlation coefficient, R ranges from zero when there is no relation, to a maximum of 1.0 when the prediction is perfect. Another useful indicator is R^2, which shows the proportion of variance in the dependent measure accounted for by the prediction equation. For instance, suppose we obtained a multiple R as large as .30. When we square the correlation, we see that $R^2 = .09$, which means that the prediction equation actually accounts for less than 10 percent of the variability in the dependent measure. We are only slightly more certain about a person's score with the predictor equation than without it. An

R of .5, on the other hand, yields an R^2 of .25, which is a substantial improvement in predictive power over no information at all.

The quality of the measure puts constraints on the predictability of the data. The Goal and Time scores are not uniformly reliable, as we have seen. It is hard to predict a score when it contains a substantial error of measurement; in fact, the reliability puts an upper limit on what we can expect to achieve in prediction.

We have not aimed toward the "best possible prediction"—a more typical approach might be to select thirty or forty predictors and try to describe a set of scores by brute force. We have selected a small number of predictors with care, based on their importance in policy for teaching training and for creation of programs.

Taking all these considerations into account, we believe that we will have done well if we succeed in predicting 25 percent of the variability in the scores in this study. This would be a useful, practical achievement—it would effectively reduce by one-half the range of individual variation in scores. For instance, the mean for the Time Average is 1.7, and the standard deviation is .33. Two-thirds of the teachers fall within a standard deviation on either side of the mean. If we know nothing at all about a teacher's situation, we would predict his responses to fall somewhere on the rating scale between 1.4 and 2.0, a range of .6. If our analysis is successful, then we can predict a Time Average rating for the individual teacher based on several predictor variables, and two-thirds of the time the teacher will depart from this prediction by only one-half of a standard deviation. For instance, if we predict the teacher's score to be 1.5, then two-thirds of the time the teacher's actual score will fall between 1.35 and 1.65, a range of .3. We can predict the teacher's judgments more accurately, and in that sense we have a better understanding of the teacher, than in the absence of any information.

Let us emphasize, our aim is not simply prediction but understanding. If we can predict accurately, we believe we will have gained a useful understanding of some of the reasons why teachers vary in their judgments about how to use time for reading instruction in the compensatory classroom. This study is not a true experiment—we cannot say for certain that the teacher spends more time on reading *because* of experience, or training, or attitude. But strong correlation suggests an influence that is worth following up. In any event, our aim is fairly accurate prediction. Let's see how well we can do.

The Predictor Variables

The predictor variables fall into three major categories—teacher experience and attitude, community background, and classroom characteristics. Table 9-3 lists the variables actually used in this analysis,

Table 9-3
Descriptive Statistics for Predictor Variables in Average Contrast Analysis
(N = 1680)

Predictor Variable	Mean	Standard Deviation
Teacher Experience and Attitude		
Years of Teaching		
1 year or less	8%	–
1 - 3 years	11%	–
3 - 6	19%	–
6 - 10	18%	–
10 - 20	27%	–
20 years or more	18%	–
Reading Training	51%	–
Believe that --		
Disadvantaged can learn		
(5=agree, 1=disagree)	3.6	.5
Disadvantaged are different		
(5=agree, 1=disagree)	3.9	.7
Student ability and attitude is poor		
(4=agree, 1=disagree)	1.2	.5
Compensatory programs are worthwhile		
(5=agree, 1=disagree)	3.3	.9
Community		
Family income ($1,000), estimated		
by principal	8.4	3.6
Class		
Grade		
2nd	37%	–
4th	34%	–
6th	25%	–
Ungraded	4%	–
Class size	28.3	15.0

arranged in the three categories, and with descriptive statistics for each measure. As you can see, we have included relatively more information about the teacher's characteristics than about the other categories, both because more information was available and because we are more interested in this aspect of the relationship. The principal's estimate of family income in the neighborhood was considered the best indicator of the community makeup. Most principals gave some response to this question—many other questions about the neighborhood were simply not answered by either teacher or principal. Poverty is known to affect students' academic performance, though the precise nature of this relation is the subject of considerable debate. We thought that poverty might also influence the teacher's goals and instructional decisions. The grade of the class has an obvious bearing on the selection of goals and the allocation of time. We included class size because it is considered by many to influence instruction, despite the generally contrary evidence (Smith, 1971; Vincent, 1969).

The descriptive statistics in Table 9-3 vary slightly from those reported elsewhere in this book because they are calculated from the subset of the data used in the regression analysis. In order for a record to be included in this analysis, it had to contain complete information about all the predictors listed in the table. The number of complete records varies slightly from one analysis to another, but generally speaking, around 1,650 of the 1,833 records were complete and included in each analysis.

There are nine predictor variables in Table 9-3. Seven of these were used directly as predictors for each of the teacher scores. Two additional predictor variables were created to answer specific questions. One question focused on the difference between the graded classes and the ungraded classes. The other question tested the departure from a linear or direct straight-line relation between years of experience and teacher scores. Specifically, we tested the hypothesis that teachers at the beginning or at the end of their careers might express different judgments than teachers in the middle of their careers, which would show up as a nonlinear effect.

An Analysis of Goals in Compensatory Reading

What determines the teacher's goals in a compensatory reading program? The relevant evidence from the multiple regression is summarized in Table 9-4. The predictor variables are listed along the left side of the table. The three Goal scores are listed across the top. Each cell contains two numbers: the first is the F-ratio, and the second is the beta weight. The statistically significant values are in bold face ($p < .01$) or italics ($p < .05$).

Goal Average. Let us look first at the Goal Average score, the filled-circle plots in Figure 9.2. Teaching experience affects this measure, as does community, family income, and the grade of the class. These relations are shown in the figure. The left-hand scale applies to the Goal Average. The influence of the predictor variables, though statistically significant,

Table 9-4
Multiple Regression Analysis of Goals Scores

	Goal Average		Readiness vs Skills		Free Reading vs Reading Skills	
	F	Beta	F	Beta	F	Beta
Teacher						
Years Teaching						
Linear Relation	**42.9**	**-.16**	2.2	-.04	–	–
Middle vs Early/Late	**14.7**	**-.09**	3.8	-.05	4.0	-.05
Reading Training	–	–	–	–	–	–
Attitude						
Believe that --						
Disadvantaged can learn						
(5=agree, 1=disagree)	–	–	4.7	-.05	**10.5**	**-.08**
Disadvantaged are different						
(5=agree, 1=disagree)	–	–	–	–	1.7	.03
Student ability and atti-						
tude is poor (5=agree,						
1=disagree)	1.8	-.03	–	–	–	–
Compensatory programs are						
worthwhile (5=agree,						
1=disagree)	3.3	.04	–	–	–	–
Community						
Family Income	**13.4**	**.09**	**17.5**	**.10**	2.8	.04
Class						
Grade 2, 4, 6 –						
Direct Relation	**14.1**	**.09**	**145.0**	**.28**	**24.8**	**12**
Grades vs Ungraded	–	–	9.5	.07	2.8	.04
Class Size	–	–	2.0	-.03	1.8	-.03
R		.26		.32		.17
R^2		.07		.10		.03

Note: F-ratios less than 1.0 and corresponding betas are not reported in this table

is not especially impressive from a practical point of view. For instance, there is a significant straight-line relation between years of teaching experience and the goal average. Teachers with more than ten years of experience judge reading as a more important goal than do teachers with

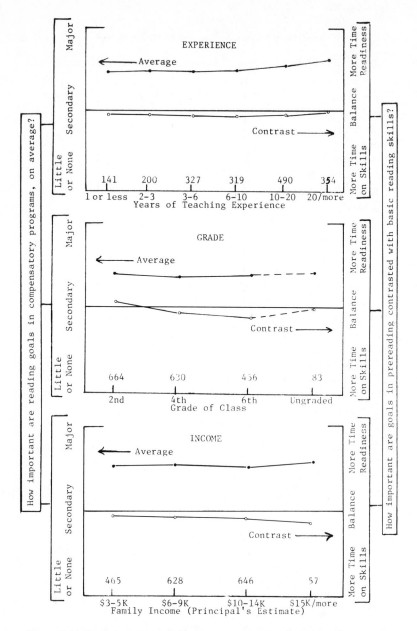

Figure 9-2/ Goal Average and Contrast scores, as a function of Experience, Grade and Family Income. Sample size is shown above abcissa.

Calfee and Drum

a single year of experience. The difference is about two-tenths of a scale value, a noticeable shift on the rather crude, three-point rating scale used here, but scarcely an enormous effect. Reading is judged a less important goal at the later grades, and as a slightly *more* important goal in higher income neighborhoods. The ratings by teachers in ungraded classes are relatively low, but the variability is 30 percent higher than for teachers of graded classes—some of the ungraded teachers think reading is very important, others think it is relatively unimportant.

Overall, the multiple regression index, R, is .26, and the total predicted variability, R^2, is only .07, a disappointing result. The predictors we have chosen tell us relatively little about why some teachers place a higher average importance on reading than other teachers. Of course, the overall rating was fairly close to the maximum possible—the typical teacher's average rating placed reading about halfway between "secondary" and "major." The ratings may be biased. Teachers know that reading is important to the parents and the community, and these teachers knew that the questionnaire focused on reading. Whatever the case, aside from the trends noted above, variations in Goal Averages are not predicted with great precision by the variables selected.

Readiness versus Skills. Looking next at the Goal Contrast for Readiness versus Skills in Table 9-4, we see that experience has little influence, but there is a large effect of grade, of the difference between graded and ungraded classes, and of the neighborhood income level. These relations are also shown in Figure 9-2 as the unfilled plots which are read on the right-hand scale.

The strongest effect is grade. Readiness is slightly favored in the second grade, but there is a strong shift toward reading skills by sixth grade. This is an expected result—what is surprising is the relatively small magnitude of the shift. The average rating for the sixth grade classes has moved toward an emphasis on advanced skills by only one-fifth of the total scale. The ungraded classes show no preference one way or the other. These compensatory classes are still focusing on quite basic skills—you might go back to the list presented earlier to remind yourself of just how basic the skills are.

The multiple regression analysis of the Goal Contrast for Readiness versus Skills produced slightly more satisfactory results than were obtained for the Goal Average scores. The R was equal to .32, and R^2 showed that 10 percent of the variance was accounted for, largely due to the strong effect of grade. It was surprising to us to find that teaching experience had so little influence on this measure. We thought that perhaps experience affected this judgment in combination with other variables, but after exploring a number of interactions found little evidence to support this idea.

Skills versus Free Reading. The contrast between Skills and Free Reading showed such weak relations with the predictor variables that we will not describe the results in any detail. The items in the free reading category were extraordinarily diverse, and we suspect that teachers interpreted them in idiosyncratic ways. With different items chosen to emphasize the contrast, more meaningful results might have been found.

Nonsignificant predictors. Finally, a few remarks about the "silent partners" in this analysis. Reading training had no consistent effect on the ratings of goals for reading instruction. To be sure, the question did not lend itself to a precise response: "Have you had any special training in the diagnosis and treatment of reading problems—yes or no?" "Special training" could presumably cover anything from a two-hour workshop to a doctorate. About half of the teachers said that they had some kind of training. The influence of "training," whatever its nature, was not so strong that it influenced the goal ratings. More detailed information on the nature and intensity of the training undergone by the teachers would have been useful as a basis for judging the value of such training over the long run.

Class size bore no relation to the goal measures. Teachers reported class sizes that ranged from one or two students to more than a hundred. The accuracy of some reports might be questioned, but we believe that most of the estimates are fairly close. It simply does not appear that class size influenced the teacher's instructional goals.

Attitudes had little effect on goals. One might think, from the literature on teacher expectancy, that the teacher who believed that disadvantaged children had little chance of benefiting from compensatory instruction would tend to give lower and more basic goal ratings—what is the sense of setting up skilled reading as a "major" goal for a group of students when you think they are unlikely to reach that goal? Nonetheless, this correlation did not appear in any direct way. Our interpretation of the finding is that the teachers tended to act quite professionally. Their beliefs about their students did not predetermine how they planned instruction. To be sure, we base this interpretation on teacher self-report, and it is some way from intention to action.

An Analysis of Time Allocation in Compensatory Reading

This study is based solely on questionnaire responses—we have no way of knowing exactly what the teachers actually did in their classes. However, we can move a bit closer to the action—the teachers were also asked how they spent their time in compensatory reading instruction. The teachers' judgments are not completely accurate measures of what happened in the classroom, but they may provide useful estimates.

The structural model. We will use multiple regression to gain an understanding of the Time scores, in a variation with some features of what is known as path analysis (Duncan, 1966). The structural model for our analysis is shown in Figure 9-3. As you can see, we propose that Time is

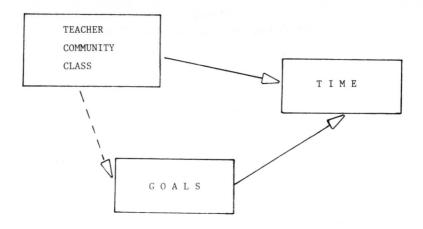

Figure 9-3. Structural model for multiple regression analysis of
     Time scores

partly determined by the direct influence of the same variables that we
selected as potential influences on Goals, but in addition, we believe that
the specific Goals of the teacher also influence Time. In using Goals as a
predictor for Time, we first take into account the influence of the background factors on the Goal scores; the specific pattern of a teacher's goals
over and above the background influences then serves as a predictor of
Time scores.

Time Average. A summary of the results of this analysis is shown in
Table 9-5. We will look first at the Time Average. Of the background
predictors, grade is most important. Teachers' judgments about how much
time was spent in compensatory reading drop about one-third in scale
value from second to sixth grade (Figure 9-4). This is a fairly large drop.
For instance, 95 percent of the second-grade teachers said they spent at
least "some" time on compensatory reading. By sixth grade, only 70
percent of the teachers spent *less* than "some" time in reading instruction.
Knowing nothing about the students, we can only guess about the rea-
sonableness of this shift—it may simply reflect the increasing competence
of the upper-grade students in this study.

The second most important predictor of the Time Average was the
amount of teaching experience. Teachers with more than ten years of
experience said they spent more time teaching reading in compensatory
programs than did teachers with less experience. The difference is noticeable, though smaller than the effect of grade. Also, you will notice that
the change with experience is not steady over years, but appears rather

Table 9-5
Multiple Regression Analysis of Time Scores

	Time Average		Readiness vs Skills	
	F	Beta	F	Beta
Teacher				
Years Teaching				
Linear Relation	26.8	-.11	24.3	-.11
Middle Years vs Early/Late	19.4	-.09	18.3	-.10
Reading Training	6.1	-.05	4.8	-.05
Attitude				
Believe that --				
Disadvantaged can learn				
(5=agree, 1=disagree)	–	–	–	–
Disadvantaged are different				
(5=agree, 1=disagree)	–	–	–	–
Student ability and attitude is poor				
(5=agree, 1=disagree)	–	–	–	–
Compensatory programs are worthwhile				
(5=agree, 1=disagree)	–	–	–	–
Community				
Family Income	8.3	.06	38.8	.17
Class				
Grade 2, 4, 6				
Direct Relation	314.6	.36	56.9	.17
Graded vs Ungraded	–	–	22.6	.10
Class Size	–	–	2.3	-.03
Goals Average	346.0	.38	23.6	.11
Goals Basic vs Advanced	–	–	249.9	.35
R	.58		.48	
R^2	.33		.23	

Note: F-ratios less than 1.0 and corresponding betas are not reported in this table

abruptly after about five years or so. Experience is correlated with age, of course, and we have no way of separating these two variables in the present study; the teachers were not asked their age.

162   *Calfee and Drum*

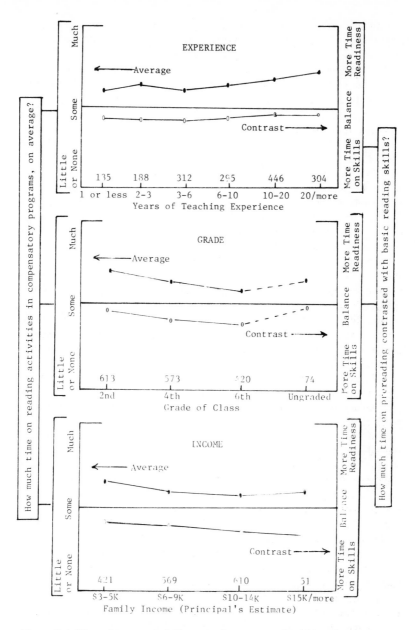

Figure 9-4. Time Average and Contrast Scores, as a function of Experience, Grade, and Family Income. Sample size is shown above abcissa.

Family income also has a slight effect on the teachers' judgments about time. In general, Time Average declines as neighborhood income goes up, but there is a slight reversal in this trend for the neighborhoods with the highest estimated income. It is important to remember that not all of the compensatory programs were in disadvantaged areas and that these data are from the early 1970s. We may be seeing the response of some teachers to the "Back to Basics" movement, which was beginning to spring up in middleclass neighborhoods at about the time of this study—we have no way of substantiating this conjecture, but it seems a reasonable possibility.

The predictors discussed to this point generate a multiple regression R of .43, and the R^2 of .19 shows that the precursor variables have a reasonably strong influence on the Time Average. However, the teacher's Goal Average also has a strong and independent effect on the Time Average. An additional 14 percent of the variance in Time Average is accounted for when we add the Goal Average to the equation. Some idea of the strength of this relation can be seen in Table 9-6. Teachers who say that reading is a major goal on Question 42 are consistent with their answer to Question 33, which asks how their pupils spend time—they spend a lot of it in reading activities. This relation shows up at every grade. As we shall see below, this is not a generalized response that "reading is fundamental." The teachers are also consistent with their goals when it comes to the specifics of how time should and should not be spent in reading activities.

Readiness versus Skills. The results of the multiple regression for the Time Contrast of Readiness versus Skills are also shown in Table 9-5. The two most important influences on this score, disregarding the teacher's goals for the moment, are grade and family income. As can be seen in Figure 9-4, the second-grade teachers say they spend slightly more time on the advanced skills, and by sixth grade the shift in this direction is quite strong, as one would expect. The ungraded teachers spend about equal time in both categories, but there are strong individual differences among these teachers—the variance in judgments in this group is about 25 percent higher than for the teachers in graded classrooms. This means that some of the ungraded teachers spend much time on skills, while others have no preference, or favor readiness.

The effects of income on the relative distribution of reading instruction is strong and consistent—teachers of low income students spend slightly more time teaching readiness, whereas teachers of students from higher income neighborhoods spend a good deal more time teaching the more advanced skills. It is important to keep in mind that all of the classes considered here have compensatory reading programs.

Finally, the single biggest influence on the Time Contrast is the Goals Contrast. The teachers who emphasize basic skills also say that they spend

Table 9-6
Percent of Teachers Spending "Lots," "Some," or "Little" time
in Reading Activities, in Each of Three Categories of
Goals—Major, Secondary, or Unimportant

	GOAL CATEGORY		
Time	Major (1.0-1.5)	Secondary (1.5-2.0)	Unimportant (2.0-3.0)
Lots (1.0 - 1.5)	42%	12%	2%
Some (1.5 - 2.0)	51%	62%	27%
Little (2.0 - 3.0)	7%	26%	71%
Number	1102	537	41

(Numbers in parentheses are rating scale values)

relatively more time on those skills, and contrariwise. Notice that the Goals Contrast is a much stronger predictor than the Goals Average. The relation between Goals and Time follow the profiles in a fairly specific way, quite apart from a general emphasis on reading per se.

Combined Effects of Predictors on Time Judgments

Next we want to look at the combined effects of the predictors on the Time scores. Up to this point, the graphs have shown the individual effects of each predictor. The influence of each separate predictor, though statistically significant, appears rather modest when considered in isolation. However, these influences work together in combination to determine the judgments of a particular teacher.

In this section we will examine how the effects operate together to produce an overall effect. We have assumed in our analysis that the effects are additive and that there are no interactions. We will also examine that assumption in this section.

Time Average. In Figure 9-5 are shown the combined effects of Goals, Grade, and Teaching Experience on the Time Average. There are two important features to this graph. One is the range from the highest to the lowest average rating in each panel. Teachers of sixth-grade classes who view reading as a relatively unimportant goal rate the time on reading in their classes at one-third of a scale unit below "some"—they spend between "some" and "little or no" time on reading, by their estimate. Second-grade teachers with more than ten years of teaching experience who set reading as a major goal rate the time the pupils spend on reading more than halfway in the direction of "a great deal" from the midpoint of "some." There is almost a full scale unit between these two extremes, on a full scale that covers only two units. Each individual predictor accounts for a modest change in teachers' ratings, but in combination the cumulative effects are quite substantial.

The second point to notice is that the effects of the predictor variables are consistent from one panel to another, with little evidence of complex interactions. The change in Time as a function of Goals is about the same at all grades; the effect of experience does not change with the teacher's goals, nor with the grade being taught. Some educational researchers have expressed concern about the complexity of educational problems (Cronbach, 1975; Campbell, 1974), and we share that concern. However, the complexity that we see arises from the joint contribution of numerous variables, not from complicated interactions among variables.

Readiness versus Skills. The parallel results for the Time Contrast of Readiness versus Skills are shown in Figure 9-6. The same generalizations mentioned earlier hold for the data in this graph. The combined effects of Grade, Goals, and Experience span more than half the distance from a slight tendency to spend more time on readiness (experienced second-grade teachers who emphasize readiness in their rating of goals) to a marked tendency to give more time to skills (fourth- and sixth-grade teachers with less than ten years' experience whose goal ratings favor skills in reading). As in the previous figure, there is no strong evidence of substantial interactions. Aside from fluctuations in data points with fewer than ten observations, the predictor variables have consistent effects on the teacher ratings.

Interactions. We did examine the data in some detail to see if interactions were occurring in other combinations of predictor variables, and found little worth reporting. A typical finding is presented in Figure 9-7, which shows for the Time Contrast score a slight interaction between Family Income and Goal Contrast. Teachers who emphasize readiness say they spend more time on readiness if they teach students from low income communities than if they teach children from middle income communities. Teachers whose Goal Contrast shows a balance between readiness and skills have the same Time scores, regardless of the family income of

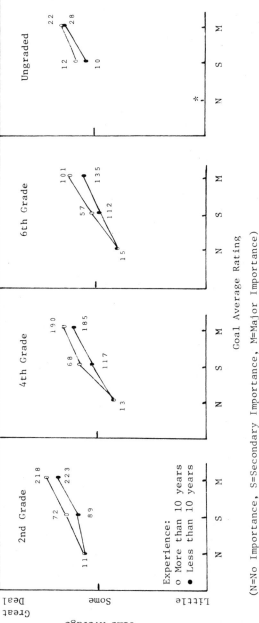

Figure 9-5. Combined effects of predictor factors on Time Average

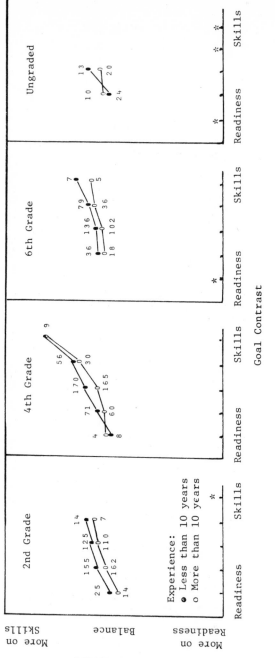

Figure 9-6. Combined effects of predictor factors on Time Contrast scores

Calfee and Drum

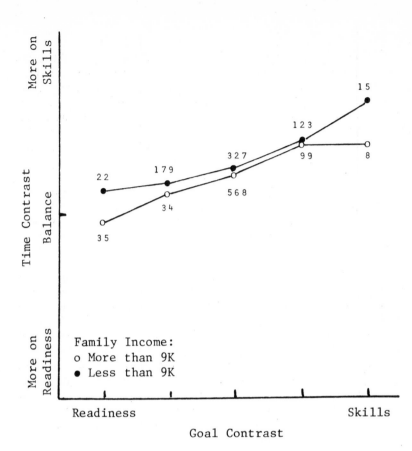

Figure 9-7. Interaction effects on Time Contrast
of Goals and Family Income

the community. (The large difference at the upper category of the Goal Contrast probably reflects the small sample size at these points.) This was one of the largest interactions we uncovered, and while it suggests a number of interesting hypotheses, we do not consider it sufficiently robust to warrant much attention.

While we are on the subject of negligible influences, we should also note that neither teacher attitude nor class size had any significant effect on the teachers' ratings of time allocated to reading. The findings for the Time scores are even less interesting than for the Goal scores. These two sets of predictors have no consistent influence on the teachers' Time ratings.

A Summary

Let us now try to summarize the results in this chapter. When the teachers' ratings of Goals and Time are averaged over all the items on these topics, we find that teachers see reading as a major goal of their programs and also seek to achieve a balance between readiness and the more advanced aspects of reading skill. The rating of Time leaves reading on the average somewhat closer to the middle of the scale and shows a relative emphasis on skills. The scales are different for Time and Goals, and the items are not equivalent, so these differences should be taken with a grain of salt.

There is considerable variation in the Goal scores, but the predictor variables selected for this analysis account for only a modest portion of the variability. It does appear that experience leads the teacher to place a higher priority on reading. Reading is also given more emphasis in the lower grades, especially advanced and free reading skills.

Ratings of the allocation of time also vary considerably, but these variations turn out to be reasonably predictable, taking into account the reliability of the summary scores. More time is spent on reading in the earlier grades, as one would expect. In the second grade there is a balance between time on readiness and skills. By the sixth grade, the pupil spends much more time on skills, according to the teacher's estimate. Experienced teachers say they spend more time on reading at all grades, and they also say they more nearly balance the time on readiness and skill development in compensatory programs. The teacher's stated goals have the single strongest influence on the time ratings—teachers are consistent in what they say is important and how they say they spend time. The effect is not a generalized "halo" effect for reading, but extends to relative allocation of time to specific skill areas. With a given content—for teachers at a particular grade, with a given level of experience, teaching children from a particular background—teachers vary markedly in their judgments about how to spend time, and these judgments are strongly related to their stated intentions about what is important to spend time on. Interestingly, training (as measured by the questionnaire) has no noticeable relation to the teachers' Goal scores, though there is a slight effect on their Time scores—intention is not influenced by training, but action is, at least weakly.

Teacher Profiles

This analysis provides an interesting profile of the teachers in compensatory reading programs. At one extreme is a teacher with a great deal of experience, who is strongly committed to reading as a goal and to the development of the basics as well as the broader reaches of the skill. This teacher spends more time with the students in the development of reading ability, in a balanced allocation of time to readiness, to the advanced skills of word analysis and comprehension, and to the freer aspects of reading—to reading in the service of thinking and creative expression of individual ideas. At another extreme is the less experienced teacher, one who does not see great importance in the teaching of reading as such. This teacher is inclined to place greater stress on the more advanced aspects of reading and to judge the basic skills as less important.

These two profiles come through clearly in the analysis, though many teachers fall between these two extremes. Let us hasten to say that we cannot place an unqualified value on one pattern or the other. To be sure, these teachers were largely identified with compensatory programs—if the students were not competent readers, then one would say that the teacher who was sensitive to this lack and arranged his priorities accordingly would be the better teacher. However, we suspect that some classes were not in need of "compensation" in the usual sense. For these students, the second profile described above might be quite appropriate. A teacher's goals and plan of instruction cannot be "right" or "wrong" in any absolute sense, but only as these meet the needs of students in a particular class. There were no items on the questionnaire about the specific instructional needs of the class, and so we cannot tell how well the teacher's profile of judgments matched the needs of the students. One item did ask the teacher what percentage of the students had previously been in compensatory reading programs. However, we found no relation between the teacher's answer to this question and the Time and Goal scores. The later phases of the Compensatory reading Study include data on student performance as well as classroom observations, and perhaps these data might shed more light on the topic.

From the present analysis, we can state that teacher's judgements do form consistent and distinctive profiles and that these are related in interesting and meaningful ways to various facets of the teacher's experience, the community, and the class. We are intrigued with the relation between goals and action in making time allocation. It would seem to us that effective training might be directed toward changing the teacher's goals, which might in turn influence action. Whatever the case, our analysis makes clear that many of the teachers who are implementing compensatory reading programs place less stress on reading as such, at all grades examined and all income levels represented in the study. We suspect that this finding might be related to the relatively low return in better reading achievement scores produced by federal and state investments in reading programs.

Chapter 10

Compensatory Reading Programs, What Are They Like, And Are They Different?

Priscilla A. Drum
University of California at Santa Barbara
Robert C. Calfee
Stanford University

The previous chapters have described the schools, the teachers, and the goals, activities, and materials of compensatory reading instruction in the early 1970s. To compensate is to make up for an existing inequity. In the instance of compensatory reading programs, the inequity springs from two sources—economic and social deprivation in the home and failure to benefit from regular classroom instruction in reading. Even today, the debate continues about the importance of these two factors for allocation of compensatory funds and the design of compensatory reading programs (OE, 1978). Below average reading achievement was the major determinant for pupil identification for placement in compensatory classes in the 1970s. The financial support for many of these classes came from the Federal government, and it is clear that poverty was the inequity of concern in Congress' enactment of Title I, the first Federal compensatory education bill:

> In recognition of the special educational needs of children of low-income families and the impact that concentration of low-income families have on the ability of local educational agencies to support adequate educational programs, the Congress hereby declares it to be the policy of the United States to provide financial assistance to local educational agencies serving areas with concentrations of children from low-income families in order to expand and improve their educational programs by various means . . . which contribute particularly to meeting the special educational needs of educationally deprived children (NIE, 1977, p. 8).

In fact, there was no real discrepancy between policy and practice. Funding was provided to local schools if they had a high proportion of low-income families, but funds allocated to a school supported programs for all the children in the school who were not making expected educational progress. Poverty and below-average educational achievement correlate. Schools in low-income neighborhoods face a multitude of burdens, and are often less able to serve the needs of their students, whether from average or below average income families.

The findings of the ETS Compensatory Reading Study provide information relevant to these policy decisions. Children from poorer families were proportionately more highly represented in compensatory reading classes than their distribution in the general school population. School staffs felt burdened by the extent of special needs, and identified the students' home background and lack of preparedness as major reasons for the low achievement. Teachers generally felt that the students could learn, but that additional resources would be required. Of course, one can debate the benefits from other allocation policies. What may be needed is additional family income rather than supplementation of the educational program (Keniston, 1977). In the 1970s, strengthening the public schools was the hope and the schools were the recipients of substantial Federal dollars. From the data provided by the ETS study, what can we say about how schools and teachers altered and augmented their reading programs during this period in order to aid children who were not making normal progress?

To answer this question requires some context, and we refer to certain other sources for comparison. First, the 1963 Austin and Morrison study examined regular reading programs and made recommendations for changes in the teaching of reading and the training of reading teachers. We examined the ETS Phase I survey to see if there was evidence that any of these recommendations were followed. Second, Southwest Regional Laboratory (SWRL) evaluated the implementation of a kindergarten reading program in over 4,000 classes in eighteen states in both 1972-73 and 1973-74. Many of SWRL's background variables—family income, ethnicity, and Title I eligibility—resemble those obtained in Phase I of the Compensatory Reading Study. There are more income categories and more ethnic divisions in the Phase I study, but the separation into poor and average incomes and into major-minority groups is virtually identical to the ETS study (Hanson & Schutz, 1975; 1976). Third, the National Institute of Education surveyed compensatory programs in a sample of one hundred schools in 1975-76 (NIE, 1977). The number of years intervening between this study and the ETS survey may seem small, but it has been a time of change, and so the comparison is worthwhile.

The Teachers

The teacher is the most powerful force in implementing the reading program. The teachers in the ETS study reported consistent patterns of goals and activities. The teachers who said that reading skills were relatively more important goals for their class were also likely to say that they spent relatively more instructional time on activities appropriate to those goals. Teacher attitudes toward their schools, their colleagues and their pupils had no noticeable effect on instructional goals and activities. This finding supports the conclusion that the teachers approached their task in a professional manner. Although many teachers felt that home conditions were an important cause of poor school achievement, the extent of these feelings bore little direct relation to the teachers' decisions about goals and activities.

Goals and instructional activities varied considerably with grade level, not surprisingly. The major effect of grade was that less time was spent on reading in the upper elementary grades. This finding may reflect the limited choices of the questionnaire—there was relatively more inquiry about basic reading activities, and only a few detailed questions about the application of reading to content areas. To be sure, many of the upper grade students may have lacked basic skill training. The survey did not ask the teacher to describe in any detail the perceived needs of the students.

Training

Austin and Morrison (1963) believed that teachers would do a better job with improved preservice and inservice training. In 1960, only 15 percent of the elementary teachers held advanced degrees. To be sure, two-thirds of the administrators said that some kind of inservice activity in reading was provided for teachers (Austin & Morrison, 1963, p. 169). By 1972, 25 percent of the teachers in compensatory classes reported that they held advanced degrees, a marked increase. Surprisingly, only 57 percent of the teachers reported special training in reading instruction beyond the initial degree. The apparent decline in "special training" may reflect the difference between asking teachers rather than principals; for instance, teachers may not consider inservice training as equivalent to advanced special instruction. The NIE survey during the 1975-76 school year showed over 30 percent of the teachers held advanced degrees, and 67 percent reported course work beyond the bachelor's degree (NIE, 1977, p. 23). The NIE survey provided no information on inservice education, but there is a widespread impression of increased inservice training in reading and language (Morrison & Austin, 1977).

Time in professional preparation does not by itself have a definite effect on practice, of course. The teachers with special training in the ETS study responded to the questionnaire about the same as those without training. Unfortunately, the "yes-no" choice to the training question reveals little about the length and character of the training, and so the absence of effect may reflect the absence of any real difference in "treatment."

Experience

Though training did not make much difference in planning compensatory reading instruction, experience did. Teachers who had taught for five or more years reported spending more time teaching reading to their students. Experience can be an excellent teacher. The thoughtful teacher sorts out what works in class from what does not. None of the other studies examined effects of experience. We would hope that future surveys might examine this factor more carefully. With declining enrollments in many American communities, experience (and age) are on the increase. It would be useful to know more about the effects of experience in dealing with various problems.

The ETS survey showed substantial reliance on classroom aides in compensatory classes—27 percent of the teachers were supported by one or more "helpers." By 1976, there was a further increase to 42 percent in aides available for compensatory reading instruction (NIE, 1977). The increased reliance on aides may reflect the principals' satisfaction with the performance of aides. The principals in the ETS survey reported that they had enough teachers but wanted more classroom aides. The reasons behind these judgments are not clear—costs may have some bearing, since two or three aides can be hired for the "price" of a certified teacher. "Districts hiring less well-educated and therefore lower paid personnel schedule more hours of compensatory instruction" (NIE, 1977, p. 36). The matter can be viewed as a cost-effectiveness decision. We know little about the actual effectiveness of aides, nor do we know anything about how teachers felt about these decisions.

We learn little about the aides from the ETS survey. What was their training and experience? What role did they play in the classroom in planning the instructional program and in carrying out instructional activities? Which students did they work with, and for what purpose? Aides are an increasingly significant element in compensatory programs, and we would hope for future surveys to provide a clearer view of the variety of individuals serving as aides and the role they play in classroom instruction.

The ETS survey did not examine the role of the "pull-out" reading specialist in classroom instruction. It appears that, in most cases, the classroom teacher supplied the major reading instruction. Over 60 percent of the teachers said that they had occasional help from a reading specialist. The type and amount of the help were not reported in the survey. Perhaps some of these activities were equivalent to the pull-out programs reported in the NIE study. We have no sure way to compare the two surveys on this point—again, we would hope that future studies, rather than looking at the instructional team as individuals, would aim toward a more comprehensive examination of the roles played by different members of the team.

The Pupils

Background

The children in compensatory programs are generally from poor families, their parents have unskilled jobs, and they are from ethnic minority backgrounds. Poverty and minority status are not direct causes of poor reading achievement, of course. At all levels of family income and educational attainment, and from all ethnic backgrounds, some children fail and some children succeed in reading achievement. However, the trends are clear in this survey, as they have been in others.

For instance, the NIE (1977) survey reported a high percentage of minority students in compensatory classes. This later survey is restricted to Title I programs, which may account for the difference—locally funded programs which were included in the ETS survey may more often serve students from middle-class neighborhoods. The Anchor Test Study (Chorvinsky, 1977) of 65,000 students from a wide range of backgrounds found strong effects of socioeconomic level and independent effects of ethnic group. The SWRL study covered a spectrum of socioeconomic levels, and about half the sample of classes was aided under Title I of ESEA. The study included measures of the entry level scores on prereading skills, the number of instructional units completed, the number of instructional days, and scores on an end-of-the-year reading test. The children were younger and the class rather than the teacher was the unit of analysis, but the entry and exit measures do allow us to examine the effects of socioeconomic status upon instructional time, amount taught, and learning outcomes. There were strong effects, which we will examine later in the chapter.

Language

One obvious link to reading achievement is the language spoken at home. Families in which English is not the primary language are disproportionately represented in compensatory reading programs. If reading instruction is in a language that the child cannot understand, it seems reasonable that the instruction will be ineffective. The Lau decision (Lau v. Nichols, 1974) is likely to change the number of children in this unhappy situation, compared to the 1970 survey. A more difficult problem is the challenge of bilingual children who have some competence in English. In the SWRL study, classes in which Spanish-surname students were in the majority performed quite poorly on the end-of-kindergarten reading test; the classes which completed less than three out of the ten instructional units did worse than any other identifiable group of students. However, those predominantly Spanish-surname classes, which completed most of the instructional units, performed as well as any other group which received a comparable amount of instruction. The slower classes may have contained relatively more students who were monolingual in Spanish; the SWRL report provided no information on language dominance.

The evidence is that many Spanish-surname students from Mexican-American and Puerto Rican backgrounds are not benefiting from reading instruction as it presently exists (NAEP, 1975). In addition to other social, economic, and cultural barriers, these children may also be confronted with a mismatch between their language and the language of the class-room. Present research and development efforts aim to remedy this situation by enhancing the teacher's skills in identifying and dealing with language variations and in providing curriculum support for a more appro-priate instructional program (Shuy, 1977; De Stefano, 1978; Politzer, 1978). The ETS survey provides little insight into this matter—neither did Austin and Morrison (1963), nor the NIE survey (1977). Given the in-creasing significance of the problem, we can expect subsequent surveys to pay it more attention.

Long-Term Needs

One other characteristic of the underachieving student comes through fairly clearly from the ETS survey—the student enters a compensatory program in the primary grades, and once he is in such a program, he tends to stay in it. According to the teachers, more than one-third of their second-graders (and about half of their fourth- and sixth-graders) had received special instruction during the preceding year. Many of the prob-lems associated with low achievement seem to have deep roots, and to require a long-term effort. If the student's home cannot support the effort to improve reading, for whatever reasons, the task of the school is likely to extend over more than a year. The ETS survey, like others on which it was modeled, considered the teacher as the unit of analysis. For the individual student, a single teacher may provide a significant learning experience, but the transitions from one class to another, from "home-room" to special class, and from reading to other subject matters—all these transitions—are part of his school life. Headstart, Follow Through, and compensatory reading programs of various sorts, all attempt to help the student for whom the odds are low for success in reading. The research evidence on transitions is hard to find—the ETS survey gives no informa-tion on this point. We suspect that many developmental activities also overlook this matter—coordination between programs for the student is seldom expressed as a central concern. We would hope that future surveys would explore this issue, and that practice would also give it some attention.

Organization of Instruction

Austin and Morrison (1963) described "a typical fourth-grade classroom, [with] thirty children whose grade equivalent scores on a standardized test ranged from 1.8 to 6.7" (p. 70). They found that students were generally sorted into three groups on the basis of their reading test scores. The teacher worked with each group in turn, using an approach and materials assumed to be appropriate for the group. Once assigned to a group, the student tended to remain with it.

Few changes appear in the decade from 1963 to 1972. The overall classroom organization for instruction in the ETS survey is remarkably similar to that reported by Austin and Morrison for regular classrooms. Average class size in the 1972 survey was 28 pupils per teacher. The teacher reported that she typically worked with two to ten students at a time. The reading groups were most often based on reading ability or the teacher's assessment of skills. More than 40 percent of the teachers reported that they rarely or never rearranged the groups. Whatever a "skill" meant, the ranking of the student's performance remained relatively constant throughout the year.

In the NIE survey, we find a substantial difference from the pattern of classroom organization reported in the earlier surveys—it may be that the meaning of compensatory instruction is not the same in the NIE study. The NIE survey found that classes "averaged 10 students in compensatory reading," and that 75 percent of the compensatory pupils were pulled out of their classrooms for special reading instruction. The instruction was most often provided by a reading specialist or by an aide. Interestingly, when the specialist gave the instruction, it lasted about three hours on the average, while instruction by an aide lasted for four and a half hours. Again, we are probably looking at a cost-effectiveness trade-off.

Instructional time was measured in the ETS, the 1972 and 1973 SWRL studies, and the 1975-76 NIE studies, though in different ways. The NIE report found that each student received "an average of 3 hours and 47 minutes per week" (p. 22) in compensatory reading instruction. The estimate from the ETS survey is closer to two and a half hours per week—half an hour a day, five days a week. These time estimates reflect the fact that the NIE study included many reading specialist programs, whereas the ETS survey focused on regular classroom teachers.

The ETS survey generally found that less time was spent on reading in the upper grades. Of the fourteen activities listed in the questionnaire, only vocabulary work and silent reading increased over the grades, and then only slightly. There was more whole group instruction, and the reading groups were larger at the later grades. All in all, the picture is one in which the opportunities for individual attention for reading instruction in the regular classroom diminish as the student moves through the grades. This pattern fits the usual trend in elementary instruction. Without special training in different procedures for classroom instruction, there is no reason why classroom teachers should depart from their usual customs during compensatory reading, and this practice appears to be what the teachers were reporting in the survey.

In the SWRL studies, records were kept of the number of instructional days, along with the number of units completed and end-of-year reading scores. Table 10-1 shows the correlations among various elements in the data structure. Descriptive statistics show the effects of socio-economic level and Title I designation on instructional days, units completed, and various reading outcomes. As can be seen in Figure 10-1, entry level, family income, and ethnic identification are all weakly but positively related to the amount of instructional time. A high-entry, middle-income, majority-culture class spent about 25 percent more days working on the reading program than a low-entry, low-income, minority-culture class. Not surprisingly, time is strongly related to number of units completed, which in turn predicts the amount learned. This result is consistent with the ETS finding that children from poorer families received more readiness instruction and less instruction on reading skills.

The most interesting feature of the SWRL study is shown in Figure 10-2. This graph shows performance on the Word Recognition test; similar results were obtained for the other outcome measures. The large amount of data displayed in the figure is overwhelming on first glance, but the significant finding appears in every panel—*test performance depends on the number of instructional units completed by a class, and is virtually independent of the entry and background characteristics of the class.* As noted earlier, a middle-income class was likely to spend more instructional days on the reading program than a lower-income class. However, the relation is not perfect—some middle-income classes completed relatively few units, and some lower-income classes completed virtually all of the instructional units. If classes are sorted on the basis of units completed, there is no effect of family income on outcome scores. This result suggests, though it does not prove, that if the amount of instruction can be controlled and equated for students from different backgrounds and different levels of ability, then reading outcomes would be controlled and equated.

Approaches and Materials

Austin and Morrison (p. 21) found that 60 percent of the school districts in their survey used a basal system as the only source for teaching reading. Another 28 percent of the districts relied on a combination of experience, charts, and basal materials; 9 percent used phonics; and only a handful reported language experience or other individualized approaches.

Table 10-1

Average Number of Days Instruction, Units Completed,
and Reading Outcomes by Income and Title I Designation
for the 1972-73 and 1973-74 SWRL Kindergarten Data

	Days		Units		Reading Outcomes	
	m	s.d.	m	s.d.	m	s.d.
Income						
< 5K						
1972–73	112	45.0	5.5	2.8	26.1	5.7
1973–74	114	32.0	5.4	2.7	27.4	4.6
Average	113	38.7	5.5	2.8	26.7	5.2
5 - 8K						
1972–73	124	38.4	6.0	2.6	28.9	7.9
1973–74	125	30.0	6.7	2.6	30.9	5.0
Average	125	34.3	6.4	2.6	29.9	6.5
8 - 12K						
1972–73	123	28.7	6.3	2.5	31.7	3.8
1973–74	128	24.9	6.7	2.4	32.5	3.8
Average	126	26.8	6.5	2.4	32.3	3.8
> 12K						
1972–73	140	16.7	7.2	2.2	34.1	3.2
1973–74	143	23.3	7.4	2.1	35.6	3.6
Average	142	20.1	7.3	2.1	35.0	3.5

Drum and Calfee

Table 10-1 (continued)

	Days		Units		Reading Outcomes	
	m	s.d.	m	s.d.	m	s.d.
Title I Designation						
Yes						
1972–73	119	37.4	5.9	3.1	29.0	4.6
1973–74	122	27.7	6.2	2.7	30.4	4.3
Average	**121**	**32.7**	**6.1**	**2.8**	**29.8**	**4.4**
No						
1972–73	127	32.1	6.4	3.3	31.6	4.4
1973–74	133	27.3	6.7	2.9	33.0	4.2
Average	**131**	**29.6**	**6.6**	**3.0**	**32.4**	**4.3**

As seen in Chapter 6, major changes in these aspects of reading instruction had occurred by the 1972 survey. Only 27 percent of the teachers said they relied solely on a basal approach. Again 9 percent reported the use of phonics, but 16 percent now carried out language experience and 25 percent had adopted some kind of individualized approach. The remaining 23 percent of the teachers reported a variety of approaches. These are substantial changes over a ten-year period, and it is natural to wonder if they are "real." The Austin-Morrison survey tapped principals' knowledge, which may be less precise than teachers'. Ten years have also seen a change in the popularity of various approaches—the teachers' description of their methods of classroom organization suggests that the actual extent of individualization was relatively modest. However, as will be mentioned below, compensatory funds have provided classroom teachers with a wider variety of materials than was available in previous years. These materials may be an important factor in producing a richer variety of methods for reading instruction.

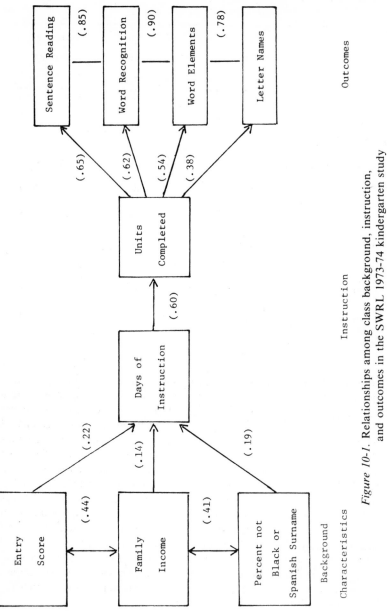

Figure 10-1. Relationships among class background, instruction, and outcomes in the SWRL 1973-74 kindergarten study

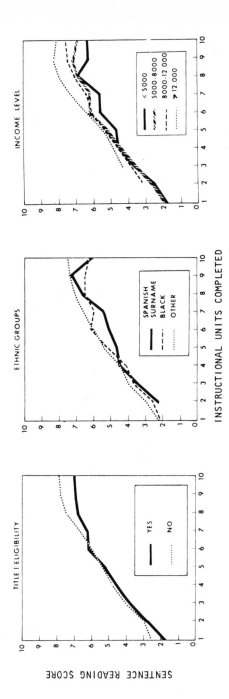

Figure 10-2. Reading performance in SWRL Kindergarten Study as a function of number of instructional units completed, Title I Eligibility, and demographic background. Except at upper levels of program, performance depends on units completed, not on background.

There remains the question of how much difference was actually realized. In Chapter 6, we found that the various approaches were not associated with differences in the rated importance of goals or time spent on classroom activities. In all approaches, comprehension was rated as the most important goal; all sought to develop favorable attitudes toward reading. Where comparisons are possible, the rankings agree with those reported in *The First R*. There was less reading aloud to the class and more work with an adult in the individualized approach, at least in the second grade.

In 1963, over 60 percent of the respondents relied on a single system of basal materials "either 'predominantly' or 'exclusively' to teach reading" (p. 54). By 1972, only 24 percent of the teachers reported that they used a single set of materials. It seems more than a coincidence that the increase in availability of a variety of materials should be associated with an increase in multiple approaches. Teachers who reported the availability of a variety of materials also were more satisfied with the materials. Does such variety help the student?—that is the critical question, of course. There is no evidence on this point in the ETS survey, but evidence from another large field study suggests that such a relation does exist (McDonald & Elias, 1976). Where the teachers had access to a rich variety of materials and used these during classroom instruction in reading (and mathematics), student achievement was enhanced. This result held for regular classrooms—it has yet to be established for compensatory programs, to the best of our knowledge.

All of these findings are consistent with Austin and Morrison's (1963, pp. 223-225) recommendations (10, 11, 14) to provide additional reading materials as supplements to basal systems. Evaluations of Title I (reported in NIE's 1977 study) have been critical of the diversion of supplemental funds to "equipment and materials rather than to educational services" (p. 5). This seems to us a superficial criticism. Where additional materials are applied for appropriate instructional purposes, they can be valuable. What works for one student may be a dud for another. Variety, if not the "spice" of classroom life, at least provides promising alternatives.

In Summary

What is the profile of the "typical" compensatory reading program of the 1970s? The ETS survey provides some trustworthy glimpses of this program, glimpses which are supported by the Austin-Morrison study (1963), the NIE report (1977), and the SWRL reports. Compensatory reading funds supported aides and extra materials, and, to an increasing degree, reading specialists. The latter gave intensive instruction to small groups. Aides decreased effective class size and increased instructional time—a cost-effectiveness analysis of these alternative resources would seem helpful. Materials increase the available variety and make it more likely that if one approach doesn't work for the student, an alternative is readily available.

Otherwise, compensatory programs resemble "regular" reading instruction, for the most part. Funds increase the *amount* of instruction, without necessarily changing the *manner*. Given the several failures to demonstrate that any particular "approach" is better than another (e.g., Bond & Dykstra, 1967; Abt Associates, 1977), this strategy seems altogether justifiable. The available research appears to show fairly consistently that differences between teachers *within* a program are greater than differences *between* programs.

There is evidence, to be sure, that "teachers make a difference" (Brophy & Good, 1974; Dunkin & Biddle, 1974; Gage, 1977). Converging evidence emphasizes the importance of class management skills—the teacher's skill at increasing student time on task, at providing appropriate questioning and feedback, and at establishing a classroom climate that promotes independence with responsibility (Duke, in press). While a considerable body of evidence supports these generalizations, opinion still carries a considerable weight when local decisions are to be made. Training materials for enhancing these skills are scattered and lack focus. Most inservice "packages" stress one particular feature or philosophy. Few can advance general and systematic evidence that generates confidence as to their validity.

Compensatory reading legislation represents a major effort to ensure equal education for all. This goal, noble though it may be, needs to be coupled with a strategy for action. One significant feature of such a strategy, in our opinion, is sound and comprehensive evaluation. We need to know what is happening in practice and which practices have payoff for students. Recent efforts in the direction of stronger and more appropriate evaluation are yielding noteworthy results (Wiley, 1977), though much remains to be done.

Another significant aspect of the strategy is the development of adequate teacher training programs. It should have been more obvious from the beginning that robust inservice training programs were essential to the success of the Title I effort, as well as other compensatory programs. Some training has been included in these programs, but it has had to compete with other needs. For instance, consider the viability of a training program in which, over a five-year interval, each member of the school faculty would be released for six months to receive specialized training for improved teaching of reading to low-achieving students. Such a program should be contrasted with the present practices of inservice training—all too often, Friday afternoon sessions listening to an expert, interspersed with an occasional weekend workshop. The more intensive, long-term program must seem "pie in the sky" to practitioners who have been on the front lines of the compensatory reading effort.[1]

Let us hasten to say, we are not proposing that the nation undertake an immediate campaign of "semi-sabbaticals" as a teacher training model. We present the idea for contrast. A massive national effort to help low-achieving youngsters has been mounted and continues to receive broad support from the Congress and the public. Central to this effort is the competence and ingenuity of the classroom teacher and the local school. The task may well call for intensive and relatively long-term training of teachers and for systematic attention to the school as an organizational unit. Without such an effort, it should not be surprising that schools and teachers combine to act as they have in the past.

It is not altogether clear to us what the model of the ideal compensatory reading program looks like. We suspect that several models are equally workable, that present practice is by no means the best for many low-performance students, and that change is needed. Changing a school is hard work, and takes skilled leadership, dedication, patience, and time (Sarason, 1971). The Federal, State, and local efforts to provide support for compensatory reading programs have benefited many students, teachers, and communities. Clear evidence for this proposition is not always easy to come by, but the general trends support the statement. Much remains to be achieved in improving the quality of compensatory reading programs. Such improvements will build upon more adequate teacher training, upon activities that enhance the integrity of schools as organizational systems, and upon assessment methods that provide a clear picture of student strengths and weaknesses. We believe that most of the elements for such improvements exist; it remains for each local school to continue to seek a pattern of elements which best fits its needs and resources.

1. The Teacher Corps as well as the new Teacher Centers provide potential models for just such an effort as we are recommending here. Both are relatively small federal efforts but can serve as exemplary models.

References

Abt Associates, Inc. *Education as experimentation: A planned variation model.* Volume IV-A: An evaluation of Follow Through, 1977. (Also published as Vol. II-A in the OE series: The Follow Through planned variation experiment.)

Anderson, R.C., Spiro, R.J., & Montague, W.E. (Eds.) *Schooling and the acquisition of knowledge.* Hillsdale, N.J.: Lawrence Erlbaum Associates, 1977.

Armbruster, F.E. The more we spend, the less children learn. *New York Times Magazine,* August 28, 1977, 9-12.

Austin, M.C., Morrison, C., & Kenney, H.J. *The torch lighters: Tomorrow's teachers of reading.* Cambridge, Mass.: Harvard University Press, 1961.

Austin, M.C., & Morrison, C. *The first R: The Harvard report on reading in elementary schools.* New York: Macmillan, 1963.

Barr, R.C. The effect of instruction on pupil reading strategies. *Reading Research Quarterly,* 1974, *10,* 555-582.

Blom, G. Sex differences in reading disability. *Reading Forum,* NINDS Monograph No. 11. Washington, D.C.: U.S. Government Printing Office, 1970, 31-46.

Bloom, B.S., Davis, A., & Hess, R. *Compensatory education for cultural deprivation.* New York: Holt, Rinehart and Winston, Inc., 1965.

Bond, G.L., & Dykstra, R. The cooperative research program in first-grade reading instruction. *Reading Research Quarterly,* 1967, *2*(4), complete volume.

Bond. G., & Tinker, M. *Reading difficulties: Their diagnosis and correction.* New York: Appleton Century Crofts, 1967.

Braun, C. Teacher expectation: sociopsychological dynamics. *Review of Educational Research,* 1976, *46*(2), 185-213.

Brody, B. Achievement of first- and second-year pupils in graded and nongraded classrooms. *Elementary School Journal,* 1970, *70,* 391-394.

Brophy, J.E., & Good, T.L. *Teacher-student relationships: Causes and consequences.* New York: Holt, Rinehart and Winston, 1974.

Bussis, A., Chittenden, E., & Amarel, M. *Beyond surface curriculum: An interview study of teacher's understandings.* Boulder, CO: Westview Press, 1976.

Calfee, R.C., Drum, P.A., & Arnold, R.D. What research can tell the reading teacher about assessment. In S.J. Samuels (Ed.), *What research has to say to the teacher of reading.* Newark, Del.: International Reading Association, 1978.

Campbell, D.T. Qualitative knowing in action research. Unpublished paper (mimeo). Stanford, CA: Stanford Evaluation Consortium, Department of Education, Stanford University, 1974.

Chaffee, J. *Beyond Serrano, paying for California's schools.* Sacramento, CA: California State Department of Education, 1977.

Chorvinsky, M. *Anchor test study: School, classroom, and pupil correlates of fifth-grade reading achievement.* National Center for Education Statistics—NCES 77-123. Washington, D.C.: U.S. Government Printing Office, 1977.

Coleman, J.S. *Equality of educational opportunity, summary report.* Washington, D.C.: U.S. Department of Health, Education and Welfare, Office of Education, 1966.

Coleman, J.S. Recent trends in school integration. *Educational Researcher,* 1975, *4,* 3-12.

Conant, E.H. *Teacher and paraprofessional work productivity: A public school cost effectiveness study.* Lexington, MA: D.C. Heath, 1973.

Cook-Gumperz, J., & Corsaro, W.A. Socio-ecological constraints on children's communicative strategies. *Sociology,* 1977, *11,* 411-434.

Coons, J.E., Clune, W.H. III, & Sugarman, S.D. *Private wealth and public education.* Cambridge, MA: Harvard University Press, 1970.

Cronbach, L.J. Beyond the two disciplines of scientific psychology. *American Psychologist,* 1975, *30,* 116-127.

Day, M.C., & Parker, R.K. *The preschool in action: Exploring early childhood programs.* Boston, MA: Allyn and Bacon, 1977.

DeStefano, J.S. *Language, the learner, and the school.* New York: John Wiley & Sons, 1978.

Deutsch, M., and Associates. *The disadvantaged child: Selected papers.* New York: Basic Books. Inc., 1967, 379-388.

Duffy, J. Project description: Teaching conceptions of reading projects. Unpublished paper (mimeo). Institute for Research on Teaching, Michigan State University, 1977.

Duke, D.L. (Ed.) *Classroom management.* Seventy-eighth yearbook of the National Society for the Study of Education. Chicago: NSSE, in press.

Duncan, O.D. Path analysis: Sociological examples. *American Journal of Sociology,* 1966, *72,* 1-16.

Dunkin, M.J., & Biddle, B.J. *The study of teaching.* New York: Holt, Rinehart and Winston, 1974.

Durkin, D. *Teaching them to read.* Boston: Allyn and Bacon, 1970.

The Elementary and Secondary Education Act of 1965.

Engle, P.L. Language medium in early school years for minority language groups. *Review of Educational Research,* 1975, *45*(2), 283-325.

Equal Employment Opportunity Commission. *1975 elementary/secondary staff information* (EEO5). Washington, D.C.: Government Printing Office, 1975.

Evans, E.D. *Contemporary influences in early childhood education.* New York: Holt, Rinehart and Winston, 1976.

Gage, N.L. Reexamination of paradigms for research on teaching. Stanford, CA: Program on Teacher Effectiveness, Center for Educational Research at Stanford, School of Education, 1977.

Golladay, M.A. *The condition of education* (1976 edition). National Center for Education Statistics, U.S. Department of Health, Education, and Welfare, NCES 76-400. Washington, D.C.: Government Printing Office, 1976.

Gonzalez, G. Teaching bilingual children. *Bilingual Education: Current Perspectives,* Vol. II. Arlington, VA: Center for Applied Linguistics, 1977, 53-59.

Goodman, K.S. A linguistic study of cues and miscues in reading. *Elementary English,* 1965, *42,* 639-643.

Grant, W.V. Education's new scorecard. *American Education,* 1972, *8*(8), 4-7.

Grant, W.V., & Lind, C.G. *Digest of education statistics.* Washington, D.C.: U.S. Department of Health, Education and Welfare, 1975.

Gray, W.S., & Rogers, B. *Maturity in reading: Its nature and appraisal.* Chicago, Ill.: University of Chicago Press, 1956.

Groff, P.J. A survey of basal reading practices. *The Reading Teacher,* 1962, *15,* 232-235.

Guthrie, J., Martuza, V., & Seifert, M. Impacts of instructional time in reading. Paper presented at Pillsbury Conference on Theory and Practice in Beginning Reading, Pittsburgh, June 1976.

Halliday, M.A.K. Language structure and language function. In J. Lyons (Ed.), *New horizons in linguistics.* New York: Penguin, 1970.

Halperin, S. ESEA ten years later. *Educational Researcher,* 1975, *4*(8), 5-9.

Hanson, R.A., & Schutz, R.E. *The effects of programmatic R&D on schooling and the effects of schooling on students: Lessons from the first-year installation of the SWRL/Ginn kindergarten program.* Technical Report 53. Los Alamitos, CA: SWRL Educational Research and Development, June 1975.

Hanson, R.A., & Schutz, R.E. *Instructional product implementation and schooling effects: Lessons from the second-year installation of the SWRL/Ginn kindergarten program.* Technical Report 56. Los Alamitos, CA: SWRL Educational Research and Development, June 1976.

Harap, H.   Many factors affect teacher morale. *The Nation's Schools,* 1959, *63*(6), 55-58.

Harris, A.J., & Morrison, C.   The CRAFT Project: A final report. *The Reading Teacher,* 1970, *22,* 335-340.

Harris, A.J., & Serwer, B.L.   The CRAFT project: Instructional time in reading research. *Reading Research Quarterly,* 1966, *2*(1) 27-56.

Harris, A.J., & Sipay, E.   *How to increase reading ability.* New York: David McKay Co., 1975.

Harste, J.C., & Burke, C.L.   A new hypothesis for reading teacher research: Both the teaching and learning of reading is theoretically based. In P.D. Pearson (Ed.), *Twenty-fifth yearbook of the National Reading Conference,* in press.

Hawkins, M.L.   Mobility of students in reading groups. *The Reading Teacher,* 1966, *20,* 136-140.

HEW.   *The effectiveness of compensatory education: Summary and review of the evidence.* Washington, D.C.: U.S. Department of Health, Education, and Welfare, 1972.

Hopkins, K.D., Oldridge, O.A., & Williamson, M.L.   An empirical comparison of pupil achievement and other variables in graded and ungraded classes. *American Educational Research Journal,* 1965, *2,* 207-215.

International Reading Association, *Professional preparation in reading for classroom teachers: Minimum standards.* Undated brochure, Professional Standards and Ethics Committee. Newark, DE: IRA.

Jones, J.C., Moore, J.W., & Van Devender, F.   A comparison of pupil achievement after one and one-half and three years in a nongraded program. *Journal of Educational Research,* 1967, *61,* 75-77.

Keniston, K., & The Carnegie Council on Children.   *All Our Children: The American family under pressure.* New York: Harcourt Brace Jovanovich, 1977.

Kerlinger, F.N., & Pedhazur E.J.   *Multiple regression in behavioral research.* New York: Holt, Rinehart and Winston, Inc., 1973.

Korth, B.   Exploratory factor analysis. In D.J. Amick & H.J. Walberg (Eds.), *Introductory multivariate analysis.* Berkeley, CA: McCutchan Publishing Corporation, 1975.

Labov, W.   The logic of nonstandard English. *Monograph Series on Language and Linguistics,* No. 22. Washington, D.C.: Georgetown University Press, 1969.

Lau vs. Nichols.   V. 414 of the U.S. Report, p. 563. Also, Supreme Court Lawyer's Edition, V.2, *D,* 1, 1974.

Machiele, R.B.   A preliminary evaluation of the non-graded primary at Leal School, Urbana. *Illinois School Research,* 1965, *1,* 20-24.

Mayeske, G.W., & Beaton, A.E.   *Special studies of our nation's students.* Washington, D.C.: U.S. Government Printing Office, 1975.

Mayeske, G.W., Wisler, C.E., Beaton, A.E., Jr., Weinfeld, F.D., Cohen, W.M., Okaha, T., Proshek, J.M., & Tabler, K.A.   *A study of our nation's schools.* Washington, D.C.: U.S. Department of Health, Education and Welfare, 1972.

McDermott, J.   Serrano: What does it mean? *Un Nuevo Dia,* 1977, *3* (Special edition), 5, 18-19.

McDonald, F.J., & Elias, P.   *Beginning teacher evaluation study: Phase II final report* (Vol. I: Ch. 10). Princeton, N.J.: Educational Testing Service, 1976.

Morrison, C., & Austin, M.C.   *The torchlighters revisited.* Newark, DE: International Reading Association, 1977.

Mulaik, S.A.   *The foundations of factor analysis.* New York: McGraw-Hill Book Co., 1972.

National Assessment of Educational Progress.   *Reading in America: A perspective on two assessments.* Denver, CO: NAEP, 1976.

National Center for Educational Statistics. *Statistics of public elementary and secondary day schools.* Washington, D.C.: U.S. Government Printing Office, 1975.

National Center for Educational Statistics. *The condition of education: A statistical report,* Vol. 3, No. 1. Washington, D.C.: U.S. Government Printing Office, 1977.

National Education Association. Status of the American public school teacher, 1970-1971. West Haven, CT: National Education Association, 1972.

National Institute of Education. *Databook: The status of education research and development in the United States.* Washington, D.C.: U.S. Government Printing Office, 1976(a).

National Institute of Education. *Evaluating compensatory education: An interim report on the NIE Compensatory Education Study.* Washington, D.C.: NIE, 1976(b).

National Institute of Education. *Administration of compensatory education.* Report of Paul Hill, Director of NIE Compensatory Education Division. Washington, D.C.: National Institute of Education, 1977.

New York State Education Department. *Which school factors relate to learning?* Albany, N.Y.: The University of the State of New York, Bureau of School Programs Evaluation, 1976.

Odden, A., et al. *School finance reform in the States 1976-1977: An overview of legislative actions, judicial decisions, and public policy research.* Denver, CO: Education Commission of the States, December 1976.

Office of Education. *Student economic background, achievement status and selection for compensatory services.* Washington, D.C.: Office of Education, Office of Planning, Budgeting and Evaluation, 1978.

Pinter, R., Eisenson, J., & Stanton, M. *The psychology of the physically handicapped.* New York: Crofts, 1941.

Politzer, R.L. Some reflections on the role of linguistics in the preparation of bilingual/cross-cultural teachers. *Bilingual Education Paper Series,* Vol. 1, No. 12. Los Angeles, CA: National Dissemination and Assessment Center, California State University, July 1978.

Ramsey, W. Reading in Appalachia. *The Reading Teacher,* 1967, *21* 57-63.

Rand Corporation. Implementing and sustaining innovations (R-1589/8-HEW). Final report in *Federal programs supporting educational change.* Santa Monica, CA: Rand Corporation, 1978.

Roeder, H.H., Beal, D.K., & Eller, W. What Johnny knows that teacher educators don't. *Journal of Research and Development in Education,* 1973, *7,* 3-10.

Rubin, D., Trismen, D.A., Wilder, G., & Yates, A. *A descriptive and analytic study of compensatory reading programs.* Phase I Report, Contract No. OEC-71-3715. Princeton, N.J.: Educational Testing Service, 1973.

Sarason, S.B. *The culture of the school and the problem of change.* Boston: Allyn and Bacon, 1971.

Searls. E.F. How to use WISC scores in reading diagnosis. *IRA reading aid series.* Newark, Delaware: International Reading Association, 1975.

Shuy, R.W. *Linguistic theory: What can it say about reading?* Newark, DE: International Reading Association, 1977.

Smith, H. Class size—does it make a difference? (Review of the Research), NCTE. Urbana, Ill.: ERIC Clearinghouse on Teaching of English, 1971.

Stallings, J.A., & Kaskowitz, D.H. Follow through classroom observation evaluation—1972-1973. Menlo Park, CA: Stanford Research Institute, 1974.

Stauffer, R. *The language-experience approach to the teaching of reading.* New York: Harper and Row, 1970.

Systems Development Corporation. Student economic and educational status and selection for compensatory education. Technical Report No. 2. Santa Monica, CA: SDC, 1978.

Tuinman, J.J. *Approaches to the teaching of reading: Why do teachers have different ways of teaching reading?* No. 3. Washington, D.C. National Reading Center Foundation, 1971.

U.S. Comptroller General. *Impact of federal programs to improve the living conditions of migrant and other seasonal farmworkers.* Washington, D.C.: U.S. Government Printing Office, 1973.

U.S. Department of Commerce, Bureau of the Census. *Educational attainment in the United States.* Series P.20-No. 284. Washington, D.C.: U.S. Government Printing Office, 1974.

U.S. Department of Commerce, Bureau of the Census. *Census of the population,* Vol. I. Washington, D.C.: U.S. Government Printing Office, 1970, p. 599.

U.S. Department of Commerce, Bureau of the Census. *Money income in 1973 of families and persons in the U.S.* Series P.60-No. 97. Washington, D.C.: U.S. Government Printing Office, 1975(a).

U.S. Department of Commerce, Bureau of the Census. *Mobility of the population of the United States, March 1970 to March 1975.* Series P-20, No. 285. Washington, D.C.: U.S. Government Printing Office, 1975(b).

U.S. Department of Commerce, Bureau of the Census. *School enrollment: Social and economic characteristics of students.* Series P-20, No. 286. Washington, D.C.: U.S. Government Printing Office, 1975(c).

U.S. Department of Commerce, Bureau of the Census. *Household money income in 1975 and selected social and economic characteristics of household.* Series P.60-No. 104. Washington, D.C.: U.S. Government Printing Office, 1977.

Veatch, J., Sawicki, F., Elliott, G., Barnette, E., & Blakey, J. *Key words to reading: The language experience approach begins.* Columbus, Ohio: Charles E. Merrill, 1973.

Vincent, W.S. Class size. In R.L. Ebel (Ed.), *Encyclopedia of educational research.* New York: Macmillan, 1969.

Wechsler, D. *Wechsler intelligence scale for children.* New York: Psychological Corporation, 1949.

Wiley, D.E. Another hour, another day: Quantity of schooling. In M. Guttentag, & Shalom Saar (Eds.), *Evaluation Studies Review Annual,* 1977, *2,* 434-476.

Wiley, D., & Harnischfeger, A. Explosion of a myth: Quality of schooling and exposure to instruction, major educational vehicles. *Educational Researcher,* 1974, *3,* 7-12.

APPENDIX
SCHOOL PRINCIPAL QUESTIONNAIRE

PART I

The first part is intended to elicit information about your school and the students in it.

1. School enrollment this year (number of pupils).

    ____ Less than 100

    ____ 100-299

    ____ 300-499

    ____ 500-699

    ____ 700-899

    ____ 900 or more

2. Number of classrooms. (Do not include offices, auditorium, or gymnasium.)

    _____

3. If you have a combination of graded and ungraded classes, indicate below the instructional organization for each grade or, if ungraded, the equivalent grades in your school. (Check only one box in each lettered row.)

Instructional Organization

Grade or Equivalent

	Check each grade *not* included in your school	Graded	Ungraded	Graded & Ungraded
a. Kindergarten	____	____	____	____
b. Grade 1	____	____	____	____
c. Grade 2	____	____	____	____
d. Grade 3	____	____	____	____

Check each grade *not*
included in your school   Graded   Ungraded   Graded & Ungraded

e. Grade 4   ___   ___   ___   ___

f. Grade 5   ___   ___   ___   ___

g. Grade 6   ___   ___   ___   ___

h. Grade 7   ___   ___   ___   ___

i. Grade 8   ___   ___   ___   ___

4. Number of classes at each grade level.

K _____   3 _____   6 _____

1 _____   4 _____   7 _____

2 _____   5 _____   8 _____

Special or
ungraded _____

5. Percentage of total student body that moved from school attendance area last year.

1. ___ 0-10%   3. ___ 26-50%   5. ___ 76-90%

2. ___ 11-25%   4. ___ 51-75%   6. ___ 91-100%

6. Percentage of total student body that moved into school attendance area last year.

1. ___ 0-10%   3. ___ 26-50%   5. ___ 76-90%

2. ___ 11-25%   4. ___ 51-75%   6. ___ 91-100%

7. Estimated percentage (this year) of pupils from families of migrant workers.

1. ___ 0-10%   3. ___ 26-50%   5. ___ 76-90%

2. ___ 11-25%   4. ___ 51-75%   6. ___ 91-100%

8. Estimated percentage of pupils whose families receive public assistance.

1. ___ 0-10%   3. ___ 26-50%   5. ___ 76-90%

2. ___ 11-25%   4. ___ 51-75%   6. ___ 91-100%

9. Estimated percentage of pupils whose head of household attained the following levels of education. (Check only one box in each lettered row.)

	0-10%	11-50%	51-90%	91-100%
a. Attended college	——	——	——	——
b. Graduated from high school but did not attend college	——	——	——	——
c. Attended but did not graduate from high school	——	——	——	——
d. Finished 8th grade but did not attend high school	——	——	——	——
e. Did not finish 8th grade	——	——	——	——

10. Estimated percentage of school families that have each of the following annual incomes. (Check only one box in each lettered row.)

	0-10%	11-50%	51-90%	91-100%
a. $12,000 and over	——	——	——	——
b. Between $9,000 and $11,999	——	——	——	——
c. Between $6,000 and $8,999	——	——	——	——
d. Between $3,000 and $5,999	——	——	——	——
e. Under $3,000	——	——	——	——

11. Estimated percentage of school families in each of the following occupational categories. (Check only one box in each lettered row.)

	0-10%	11-50%	51-90%	91-100%
a. Professionals (doctors, lawyers, etc.)	——	——	——	——
b. Business owners or managers	——	——	——	——
c. White collar workers (clerks, salespersons, etc.)	——	——	——	——
d. Skilled workers; farm owners	——	——	——	——
e. Unskilled, farm, or service workers	——	——	——	——
f. Unemployed	——	——	——	——

12. Estimated percentage of students of the following racial or national origins. (Check only one box in each lettered row.)

	0-10%	11-50%	51-90%	91-100%
a. Caucasian or White	____	____	____	____
b. Negro or Black	____	____	____	____
c. Spanish surnamed	____	____	____	____
d. Oriental	____	____	____	____
e. American Indian	____	____	____	____
f. Other (specify _____)	____	____	____	____

13. Are children bused to your school from other neighborhoods not in your school's regular attendance area?

1. ____ Yes

2. ____ No

14. If children are bused in, about what percentage of the total student body is bused in?

1. ____ 0-10%   3. ____ 26-50%

2. ____ 11-25%   4. ____ More than half

15. Are children bused from your school's attendance area to schools in other neighborhoods?

1. ____ Yes

2. ____ No

16. Using your best professional judgment, rate each of the following characteristics for your school.

	Highly Adequate	Adequate	Inadequate	Highly Inadequate
Size of physical plant for pupil	____	____	____	____
Condition of physical plant	____	____	____	____
Suitability of physical plant for program operation	____	____	____	____
Number of instructional personnel	____	____	____	____
Number of other professional personnel	____	____	____	____
Number of teacher aides	____	____	____	____
Number of other nonprofessionals	____	____	____	____

Quantity of books, periodicals, and other printed materials	___	___	___	___
Suitability (quality) of books, periodicals, and other printed materials for instruction	___	___	___	___
Quantity of audiovisual materials	___	___	___	___
Suitability (quality) of audio-visual materials for instruction	___	___	___	___
Quantity of instructional equipment	___	___	___	___
Suitability (quality) of instructional equipment for instruction	___	___	___	___

17. Estimate the percentage of students in your school at each of the following grade levels who are reading one or more years below grade level according to current test data. The estimate should be based upon the concept of national norms for the grade for which you are reporting.

    a. Grade 2   b. Grade 4   c. Grade 6

18. Are there students in your school who in your judgment are in need of remedial reading instruction but who are not receiving such instruction?

    1. ___ Yes

    2. ___ No

If no, go on to Question 19.

    a. If yes, how many students?

    b. If yes, how many students are there in need of remedial reading instruction in each of the following grades?

        1. ___   4. ___   7. ___

        2. ___   5. ___   8. ___

        3. ___   6. ___   Ungraded ___

PART II

This part of the questionnaire is intended to elicit information about the compensatory reading program(s) in your school. By compensatory reading instruction is meant any reading instruction provided to students because they are reading below their grade level.

19. Does your school conduct at least one compensatory reading program as defined?

        1. ___ Yes If so, please go on to question 21 and complete the remainder of this questionnaire. At the same time, please distribute questionnaires in the manner prescribed below.

2. ____ No   If not, DO NOT COMPLETE THIS QUESTIONNAIRE.
HOWEVER, PLEASE ARRANGE FOR TEACHER QUES-
TIONNAIRES TO BE COMPLETED BY *ONE* TEACHER
OF *EACH* OF GRADES 2, 4, AND 6 (3 teachers in all)
HAVING THE CLASS WITH THE LOWEST AVERAGE
READING ACHIEVEMENT. These teachers should receive
Teacher Characteristics Questionnaires (tan) and Class and
Program Characteristics Questionnaires (yellow).

20. How many separate and distinct compensatory reading programs are currently
operating in your school? (Include teacher training programs conducted during
the summer preceding the current school year.)

   ____ One   ____ Four

   ____ Two   ____ More than four

   ____ Three

21. Are any of the compensatory reading programs in your school funded totally
or in part by funds (federal, state, local, or other) *supplementary to the regular
ongoing school budget?*

   ____ Yes

   ____ No
                    }   If No or Don't know, skip to question 22.
   ____ Don't know

21a. When was the first compensatory reading program funded by supplementary
sources made available in your school?

   ____ One year ago

   ____ More than 1 but less than 2 school years ago

   ____ More than 2 but less than 3 school years ago

   ____ Three or more school years ago

   ____ Don't know

22. How long has (have) the present compensatory reading program(s) been
available in your school? (Answer separately for each program.)

	Program 1	Program 2	Program 3	Program 4
One school year or less	____	____	____	____
More than 1 but less than 2 school years	____	____	____	____
More than 2 but less than 3 school years	____	____	____	____
Three or more school years	____	____	____	____

23. What was your school per pupil expenditure last year?

_____ ____ Check here if you don't know

24. What was your district per pupil expenditure last year?

_____ ____ Check here if you don't know

25. What are the *total* funds allocated for compensatory reading in your school?

_____ ____ Check here if you don't know

26. What are the costs per pupil of compensatory reading in your school?

_____ ____ Check here if you don't know

27. If there are separate compensatory reading programs in your school, please provide the following breakdown(s) of costs by program and by component parts.

	Program 1	Program 2	Program 3	Program 4
Total cost of program				
Cost of personnel: Professional				
Other				
Cannot break down cost(s) for program (Check)				

28. How many pupils participate in (each of the) compensatory reading programs in your school? (If there is more than one program answer separately for each. If individual children participate in more than one program, count them in each total.)

Number of Pupils

Program 1 _____

Program 2 _____

Program 3 _____

Program 4 _____

29. Approximately what percentage of the pupils at each grade level in your school participate in the compensatory reading program(s)? (Answer separately for each program.) If classes are ungraded, answer using number of years in school instead of grade level and check this box _____ .

Grade	PROGRAM 1				PROGRAM 2				PROGRAM 3				PROGRAM 4			
	0	1-25	26-50	51-100	0	1-25	26-50	51-100	0	1-25	26-50	51-100	0	1-25	26-50	51-100
K	—	—	—	—	—	—	—	—	—	—	—	—	—	—	—	—
1	—	—	—	—	—	—	—	—	—	—	—	—	—	—	—	—
3	—	—	—	—	—	—	—	—	—	—	—	—	—	—	—	—
4	—	—	—	—	—	—	—	—	—	—	—	—	—	—	—	—
5	—	—	—	—	—	—	—	—	—	—	—	—	—	—	—	—
6	—	—	—	—	—	—	—	—	—	—	—	—	—	—	—	—
7	—	—	—	—	—	—	—	—	—	—	—	—	—	—	—	—
8	—	—	—	—	—	—	—	—	—	—	—	—	—	—	—	—

30. About what percentage of the students participating in each of the compensatory reading programs in your school are from culturally, linguistically, and/or economically deprived backgrounds? (Mark one box in each lettered row.)

	0-10%	11-50%	51-90%	91-100%	Don't know
a. Program 1	——	——	——	——	——
b. Program 2	——	——	——	——	——
c. Program 3	——	——	——	——	——
d. Program 4	——	——	——	——	——

31. Indicate below the actual numbers of classes and pupils in the compensatory reading program(s) at each of the specified grade levels in your school. (Answer for all programs combined.) If classes are ungraded, answer using number of years in school instead of grade level and check this box _____ .

	Total for School	Total for Grades		
		2	4	6
Number of class sections	_____	____	____	____
Number of students	_____	____	____	____

32. Indicate the approximate level of funding for the compensatory reading program(s) in your school by each source indicated below: (Answer separately for each program.)

	PROGRAM 1	PROGRAM 2	PROGRAM 3	PROGRAM 4
	Total / Partial / None	Total / Partial / None	Total / Partial / None	Total / Partial / None
Federal ESEA Title I	— — —	— — —	— — —	— — —
Other (specify)	— — —	— — —	— — —	— — —
_____	— — —	— — —	— — —	— — —
State (specify)				
_____	— — —	— — —	— — —	— — —
Local (specify)				
_____	— — —	— — —	— — —	— — —
Other				
_____	— — —	— — —	— — —	— — —

____ Check here if you cannot provide information requested in question 32.

33. Was any teacher resistance encountered in the implementation of the compensatory reading program(s) in your school?

     ____ None at all

     ____ Some

     ____ A great deal

34. Was any community resistance encountered in the implementation of the compensatory reading program(s) in your school?

     ____ None at all

     ____ Some

     ____ A great deal

35. What is the basis for determining pupil participation in the compensatory reading program? *(Mark all that apply.)*

     ____ All students in the school participate

     ____ Membership in one or more specific target groups (i.e., economically disadvantaged, migrants, non-English speaking)

     ____ Depressed reading levels (as indicated by test results)

_____ Teacher (or other staff) recommendation

_____ Parent request

_____ Volunteer

_____ Other (specify) _____

36. Since June 1971, how many and what types of personnel in your school have participated in inservice training activities to prepare them for teaching in a compensatory reading program for elementary students?

Number of
individuals

_____ Regular classroom teachers

_____ School located reading specialists

_____ School district reading specialists

_____ School personnel other than above (specify) _____

_____

37. Does the compensatory reading program use parents or other volunteers (paid or unpaid) to help in the classroom?

1. _____ Yes

2. _____ No

38. Does the compensatory reading program use pupils as tutors?

1. _____ Yes

2. _____ No

39. Do you expect to have a compensatory reading program in the summer of 1973?

1. _____ Yes

2. _____ No

3. _____ Don't know

40. If you do expect to have a summer program, for which of the following grades will the program be conducted. (Circle all that apply.)

K   1   2   3   4   5   6   7   8   Ungraded

40a. On what basis do you expect to select students for the summer program? *(Check all that apply.)*

   ____ Previous participation in a compensatory reading program

   ____ Previous *non*participation in a compensatory reading program

   ____ Depressed reading level

   ____ Membership in one or another specific target groups (economically deprived, etc.)

   ____ Teacher or other staff recommendation

   ____ Parent request

   ____ Volunteer

   ____ Other (specify) _____

SURVEY OF COMPENSATORY READING PROGRAMS
TEACHER CHARACTERISTICS QUESTIONNAIRE

1. What is your sex?   _____ Male   _____ Female

2. How many years of teaching experience (public and nonpublic), including this school year, have you had?

   ____ One year or less

   ____ More than 1 year but less than 3 years

   ____ At least 3 years but less than 6 years

   ____ At least 6 years but less than 10 years

   ____ At least 10 years but less than 20 years

   ____ Twenty years or more

3. How many years, including this school year, have you taught in this school?

   ____ One year or less

   ____ More than 1 year but less than 3 years

   ____ At least 3 years but less than 6 years

   ____ At least 6 years but less than 10 years

_____ At least 10 years but less than 20 years

_____ Twenty years or more

4. What type of teaching certification do you have?

     _____ No certificate

     _____ Temporary, provisional, or emergency certification

     _____ Regular certification

5. What is the highest earned college degree you hold? (Do not report honorary degrees.)

     _____ No degree

     _____ A degree or diploma based on less than 4 years of work

     _____ A bachelor's degree

     _____ A master's degree

     _____ A doctor's degree (EdD, PhD, etc.)

6. Have you had any special training in the diagnosis and treatment of reading problems?

     _____ Yes   _____ No

  a. If yes, at what academic level was the training?

     _____ Undergraduate

     _____ Graduate

     _____ Inservice

     _____ On the Job

     _____ Other (specify)   _____

7. Are most of your students of the same racial or national origin as you?

     _____ Yes   _____ No

8. Were you assigned to or did you choose the school in which you are teaching?

     _____ Was assigned to school   _____ Chose school

9. Were you assigned to or did you choose to teach the class you are teaching this year?

     _____ Was assigned to class   _____ Chose class

The questions that follow are all designed to elicit your opinions about your school, the pupils you teach, and any compensatory reading program you might be involved in. Please answer the questions as candidly as you are able. There are no "right" answers to these questions; we are interested in obtaining some information about how teachers feel about compensatory reading programs and about the pupils in them.

10. Compared with other elementary schools in your district or community, how satisfied are you with respect to the following things about your school?

	Highly Satisfied	Moderately Satisfied	Moderately Dissatisfied	Highly Dissatisfied
Physical facilities (buildings, etc.)	——	——	——	——
Faculty (teachers)	——	——	——	——
Ability of student body	——	——	——	——
Attitudes of student body	——	——	——	——
Administration	——	——	——	——
Overall philosophy of education	——	——	——	——

11. How responsive is the administration of your school to any requests you might make for additional teaching materials or equipment?

____ Highly responsive

____ Moderately responsive

____ Not at all responsive

12. For remedial or other help for one of your students?

____ Highly responsive

____ Moderately responsive

____ Not at all responsive

13. For changes in your curriculum?

____ Highly responsive

____ Moderately responsive

____ Not at all responsive

14. Do you believe there is a sound basis in educational policy for giving compensatory programs to disadvantaged students at extra cost per pupil?

     ____ Definitely yes

     ____ Probably yes

     ____ I am undecided

     ____ Probably no

     ____ Definitely no

15. Do you believe that compensatory programs are generally worthwhile?

     ____ Definitely yes

     ____ Probably yes

     ____ I am undecided

     ____ Probably no

     ____ Definitely no

16. The following statements are all related to the academic capabilities of disadvantaged pupils. For each statement, indicate the degree to which you agree or disagree with the idea expressed.

		Strongly Disagree	Disagree	Uncertain	Agree	Strongly Agree
a.	With proper instruction they can learn about as well as any other pupils.	____	____	____	____	____
b.	No matter how good the instruction these pupils receive they will always score lower than middle class children.	____	____	____	____	____
c.	These children do not want to learn.	____	____	____	____	____
d.	The pupils want to learn but they do not have the right background for school work.	____	____	____	____	____
e.	It has been sufficiently proven that such pupils will never do as well as other students.	____	____	____	____	____
f.	Materials are more important than methods in the teaching of reading.	____	____	____	____	____

Appendix

		Strongly Disagree	Disagree	Uncertain	Agree	Strongly Agree
g.	Methods are more important than materials in the teaching of reading.	—	—	—	—	—
h.	The teacher's ability is more important than either method or materials in the teaching of reading.	—	—	—	—	—
i.	Disadvantaged children have more trouble learning to read than advantaged children.	—	—	—	—	—
j.	Disadvantaged children have a shorter attention span than advantaged children.	—	—	—	—	—
k.	Disadvantaged children have different linguistic experiences than advantaged children.	—	—	—	—	—
l.	Disadvantaged children are disadvantaged mainly in that they do not have the foundation of concepts that advantaged children have.	—	—	—	—	—
m.	Learning to verbalize complete thoughts is particularly important for disadvantaged children.	—	—	—	—	—
n.	Improving the student's self-image as a learner is particularly important for disadvantaged children.	—	—	—	—	—
o.	The ability to ask questions which require a complete answer is extremely important in teaching reading to disadvantaged children.	—	—	—	—	—
p.	In teaching reading, a wrong response can be as useful as a correct response.	—	—	—	—	—
q.	Disadvantaged children often have lower aspirations than advantaged children.	—	—	—	—	—

Appendix

207

SURVEY OF COMPENSATORY READING PROGRAMS
CLASS AND PROGRAM CHARACTERISTICS QUESTIONNAIRE

I. CLASS CHARACTERISTICS

If you are a classroom teacher, answer questions 1 and 2. If you are *not* a classroom teacher, skip to question 3.

1. What grade do you teach?

    ____ Two

    ____ Four

    ____ Six

    ____ Ungraded

1a. How many pupils are in your class? (Give actual number)   _____

How many are boys?   _____

How many are girls?   _____

2. How many of the pupils in your class receive compensatory reading instruction as defined above?

    ____ All of the pupils in my class receive compensatory reading instruction

    ____ from me

    ____ some from me and some from another teacher

    ____ Selected pupils in my class receive compensatory reading instruction

    ____ from me

    ____ some from me and some from another teacher

3. The following questions refer *only* to those pupils who receive their compensatory reading instruction from you. If you *do* teach compensatory reading to

    more than one class, indicate in the box how many classes you teach.   _____

    How many pupils receive compensatory reading instruction from you? (Include any pupils who may be sent to your classroom especially for compensatory reading instruction.)

    Total number of pupils   _____

    a. How many are boys?   _____

    b. How many are girls?   _____

4. What is the age range of the children in your compensatory reading class?

Age of oldest child _____/_____ Age of youngest child _____/_____

                                 Years   Months   Years   Months

5. What percentage of the pupils in your compensatory reading class have received compensatory reading instruction prior to this year?

    ____ None

    ____ 1-25%

    ____ 26-50%

    ____ 51-75%

    ____ 76-100%

    ____ Don't know

6. About what percentage of the children in your compensatory reading class attended some form of school? (Include Headstart, day care, or nursery school; *do not include public school kindergarten.*)

    ____ None

    ____ 1-25%

    ____ 26-50%

    ____ 51-75%

    ____ 76-100%

    ____ Don't know

7. About what percentage of the pupils in your compensatory reading class are members of the following racial or national origin groups? (Mark *one* box in *each* lettered row.)

	None	1-25%	26-50%	51-75%	76-100%
a. Caucasian or White	____	____	____	____	____
b. Negro or Black	____	____	____	____	____
c. Spanish surnamed	____	____	____	____	____
d. Oriental	____	____	____	____	____
e. American Indian	____	____	____	____	____
f. Other (specify)	____	____	____	____	____

_____

8. Estimate the percent of the pupils in your compensatory reading class who are from homes in which the dominant language is not English.

     ____ None

     ____ 1-25%

     ____ 26-50%

     ____ 51-75%

     ____ 76-100%

     ____ Don't know

8a. Among the homes where the dominant language is not English, what language(s) is (are) spoken? (Mark all that apply.)

     ____ American Indian

     ____ Chinese

     ____ Japanese

     ____ Spanish-Portuguese

     ____ French

     ____ Other (specify)   _____

9. Estimate the percentage of pupils in your compensatory reading class who have persistent problems in each of the following areas. (Mark *one* box in each lettered row.)

	None	1-10%	11-50%	51-100%	Don't know
a. Speech	____	____	____	____	____
b. Vision	____	____	____	____	____
c. Hearing	____	____	____	____	____
d. Frequent illness	____	____	____	____	____
e. Mental retardation	____	____	____	____	____
f. Emotional problems	____	____	____	____	____
g. Family instability	____	____	____	____	____
h. Other (specify)	____	____	____	____	____

_____

10. Estimate the percentage of pupils in your compensatory reading class whose family incomes are derived from each of the following occupational categories. (Mark *one* box in each lettered row.)

	None	1-10%	11-50%	11-50%	91-100%
a. Unskilled or service workers	____	____	____	____	____
b. Skilled workers or farm owners	____	____	____	____	____
c. White collar workers (clerks, salespeople, etc.)	____	____	____	____	____
d. Business owners or managers	____	____	____	____	____
e. Professionals (doctors, lawyers, etc.)	____	____	____	____	____
f. Unemployed	____	____	____	____	____
g. Don't know	____	____	____	____	____

11. What is the average absentee rate in your compensatory reading class? (About what percentage of the class is absent on any given day?)

____ 0-10%

____ 11-20%

____ 21-30%

____ 31-40%

____ 41-50%

____ More than 50%

12. Which of the following would you judge to be the major causes of absenteeism among your pupils? (Mark yes or no for each cause.)

1 Yes	2 No	
____	____	Illness of pupil
____	____	Illness of other family member(s)
____	____	Lack of parental concern

_____ _____ Need for pupil to perform other duties at home

_____ _____ Suspension or expulsion

_____ _____ Other (specify)   _____

13. Estimate the percentage of your pupils whose families have moved into this school attendance area during the school year.

_____ None

_____ 1-25%

_____ 26-50%

_____ 51-75%

_____ 76-100%

_____ Can't estimate

14. Estimate the percentage of your pupils who have moved out of the school attendance area this year.

_____ None

_____ 1-25%

_____ 26-50%

_____ 51-75%

_____ 76-100%

_____ Can't estimate

Questions 15 and 16 ask for your *opinions* about the pupils you teach. Please answer the questions as candidly as you are able; there are no "right" answers.

15. How far do you expect the average pupil in your compensatory reading class would be able to go in school if he were given the opportunity?

_____ Eighth grade, or lower

_____ Ninth, tenth, or eleventh grade

_____ High school graduate

_____ Junior college, business school, or some other postsecondary course, but not a four year college

_____ Four year college or beyond

_____ Other (specify)   _____

16. How far do you expect the average pupil in your compensatory reading class *will* actually *go* in school?

    ____ Eighth grade, or lower

    ____ Ninth, tenth, or eleventh grade

    ____ High school graduate

    ____ Junior college, business school or some other postsecondary course, but not a four year college

    ____ Four year college or beyond

    ____ Other (specify) _____

II. PROGRAM CHARACTERISTICS

If you *do* teach more than one class, check this box. _____

If you teach in more than one program, check this box. _____

17. When is compensatory reading instruction carried out? (Check all that apply.)

    ____ During regular school hours in time scheduled for regular reading instruction

    ____ During regular school hours in time released from other class work

    ____ Before or after school or on weekends

    ____ During the summer

    ____ Other (specify) _____

18. If compensatory reading instruction is carried on in time released from other class work, which of the following subject matter areas receive correspondingly reduced time? (Mark all that apply.)

    ____ Social Studies

    ____ Science

    ____ Mathematics

    ____ Foreign Language

    ____ Language Arts

    ____ Physical Education

_____ Art

_____ Music

_____ Seat work, study time, etc.

_____ Other (specify) _____

19. What is the average amount of formal instruction time per student in compensatory reading?

   a. Minutes per instructional period

   _____ 1-15

   _____ 16-30

   _____ 31-40

   _____ 41-50

   _____ 51-60

   _____ 61-75

   _____ 76-90

   _____ 91 or more

   b. Number of instruction periods per week

   _____ One

   _____ Two or three

   _____ Four or five

   _____ More than five

20. Do most pupils receive compensatory reading instruction at the same time of day every instructional day?

   1. _____ Yes

   2. _____ No

   a. If yes, when is the instructional period?

   _____ Before school

   _____ Morning (before lunch)

   _____ Afternoon (after lunch)

   _____ After school

214

b. If no, when does instruction take place?

_____ Mostly in the morning

_____ Mostly in the afternoon

_____ About equally divided between mornings and afternoons

21. What additional personnel are available to you in your teaching of compensatory reading?

	Frequently	Occasionally	Rarely	Not Available
Remedial reading teacher or supervisor	——	——	——	——
Other professionals (counselors, psychologists, etc.)	——	——	——	——
Paraprofessionals or teacher aide	——	——	——	——
Parent or other volunteer	——	——	——	——
Student teacher	——	——	——	——
Media specialist	——	——	——	——
Resource teacher (music, art, etc.)	——	——	——	——
Older student in school	——	——	——	——
Other (specify) _____	——	——	——	——

22. During the school year, how many teachers other than yourself have held your particular teaching assignment with your compensatory reading class for at least *two consecutive weeks?* Count substitute teachers and replacement teachers; do *not* count student teachers or classroom aides.

_____ None

_____ One

_____ Two

_____ Three

_____ More than three

23. If your compensatory reading class is organized into groups, indicate the frequency with which you organize these groups by each of the following criteria.

	Frequently	Occasionally	Rarely	Never
Reading grade level	____	____	____	____
Specific skill deficiencies	____	____	____	____
Shared interests	____	____	____	____
Specific projects	____	____	____	____
Other (specify) _____ ____		____	____	____

24. How often do the following instructional groups operate (occur) in the course of your teaching of compensatory reading?

	All of the time	Frequently	Occasionally	Rarely or Never
Adult and child in one-to-one relationship	____	____	____	____
Adult and children in groups of between 2 and 10	____	____	____	____
Adult and children in groups of between 11 and 20	____	____	____	____
Adult and children in groups of more than 20 (includes whole class instruction)	____	____	____	____
Individual pupils working independently	____	____	____	____
Pupil teams working independently	____	____	____	____
Other (specify) _____	____	____	____	____

25. If your compensatory reading class is organized into groups, about how frequently does the composition of the group change?

____ Daily

____ Weekly

____ Biweekly

____ Monthly

_____ Rarely, if ever

_____ Other (specify) _____

26. In a sentence or two, describe the outstanding features of your compensatory reading program.

27. Which one of the following terms comes closest to describing your major classroom approach to the teaching of compensatory reading?

      _____ Linguistic-phonetic

      _____ Language experience

      _____ Modified alphabet

      _____ Eclectic

      _____ Other (specify) _____

28. How long have you used this method?

      _____ This is the first year

      _____ For one or two years

      _____ For three, four, or five years

      _____ For six years or more

29. To what extent do you use each of the following approaches to teaching compensatory reading in your classroom?

	Not at All	Minimally	Somewhat	Extensively
Basal readers	_____	_____	_____	_____
Programed instruction	_____	_____	_____	_____
A total phonics program	_____	_____	_____	_____
A supplementary phonics program	_____	_____	_____	_____
Language experience	_____	_____	_____	_____
A linguistic program	_____	_____	_____	_____
Nonstandard orthography (i.t.a.)	_____	_____	_____	_____

Words in Color   ____   ____   ____   ____

Individualized programs   ____   ____   ____   ____

Technological devices
such as the "talking
typewriter" or
teaching machines   ____   ____   ____   ____

Other (specify and
describe)   ____   ____   ____   ____

30. Who selected the materials that you are currently using in your teaching of compensatory reading?

    ____ You, and you alone

    ____ You, as a member of a team or committee

    ____ An individual who asked for your views; or a team or committee of which you were not a member but on which your views were represented

    ____ An individual, team, or committee, operating without any input from you

    ____ Other (specify) _____

31. How satisfied are you with the materials you are currently using in your teaching of compensatory reading?

    ____ Totally satisfied

    ____ Satisfied in major aspects; dissatisfied in some minor ones

    ____ Lukewarm; neither devoted nor opposed to the materials

    ____ Dissatisfied in major aspects; satisfied only in some minor ones

    ____ Totally dissatisfied

32. How frequently do you use the following materials in the course of your compensatory reading instruction?

	Not Available	Often	Sometimes	Rarely or Never Use
Textbooks other than basal readers	____	____	____	____
Books and printed materials other than textbooks	____	____	____	____

Newspapers, magazines,
and other periodicals   ___   ___   ___   ___

Teacher prepared
materials (dittos, etc.)   ___   ___   ___   ___

Motion pictures and/or
filmstrips   ___   ___   ___   ___

Slides and transparencies   ___   ___   ___   ___

Tape recordings and
records   ___   ___   ___   ___

Video or television tapes   ___   ___   ___   ___

Games, puzzles, and toys   ___   ___   ___   ___

Other (specify) _____   ___   ___   ___   ___

33. How much time does a typical pupil in your compensatory reading class spend
    in each of the following types of activity?

	A great deal	Some	Little or none
Improving motor abilities related to reading	___	___	___
Increasing attention span	___	___	___
Developing visual discrimination	___	___	___
Matching letters or words	___	___	___
Learning letter forms	___	___	___
Developing a sight vocabulary (whole word recognition)	___	___	___
Learning word meanings (vocabulary)	___	___	___
Phonic and/or structural analysis	___	___	___
Being read to	___	___	___
Reading aloud	___	___	___
Reading silently (independent silent reading)	___	___	___
Creative writing	___	___	___

Reading for enjoyment ___ ___ ___

Enriching cultural background ___ ___ ___

Other (specify) _____ ___ ___ ___

34. Have you had any special training in the teaching of reading or in instructional techniques for disadvantaged pupils in connection with your current teaching assignment?

    1. ___ Yes

    2. ___ No

If no, skip to question 39.

If yes, please answer questions 35-38.

35. What form did the special training take? (Check all that apply.)

    ___ Summer workshop or institute

    ___ College course (whether or not for degree credit)

    ___ After school or weekend workshop(s)

    ___ Released time workshop(s)

    ___ Individual instruction with supervised practice teaching

    ___ Other (specify) _____

36. Which of the following areas were explored in the course of the special training you recieved? (Check all that apply.)

    ___ New instructional techniques in reading

    ___ Diagnosis of reading problems

    ___ Open classroom methods

    ___ Individualized instruction

    ___ Use of equipment and materials

    ___ Techniques for cultural enrichment

    ___ Other (specify) _____

37. Over what time period did the special training extend?

    ___ One summer

    ___ One academic semester

_____ One academic year

_____ One calendar year

_____ One summer and one academic year

_____ Other (specify) _____

38. How long ago did you receive your special training?

     _____ Less than one year ago

     _____ More than one but less than two years ago

     _____ More than two but less than three years ago

     _____ Three or more years ago

39. For a typical pupil in your compensatory reading program, about how much in-school time is devoted to each of the following reading or reading related activities?

	None	Less than 1 hour/week	Between 1 and 4 hours/week	More than 1 hour a day (5+ hours/week)
Basic reading instructional program	_____	_____	_____	_____
Compensatory reading	_____	_____	_____	_____
Instructional program (only if compensatory reading program is different from basic instructional program)	_____	_____	_____	_____
Reading in content areas (science, social studies, etc.)	_____	_____	_____	_____
Independent (self-selected) reading	_____	_____	_____	_____
Library activities	_____	_____	_____	_____
Enrichment activities (trips, special assemblies, etc.)	_____	_____	_____	_____
Other relevant activities (specify) _____	_____	_____	_____	_____

40. Please indicate below what materials you use in your compensatory reading instruction and to what extent you use them.

	Series Titles (specify)	Use as major resource in teaching reading	Use as supplemental or optional course in class	Occasionally refer to myself but don't use in class	Don't use at all
Scott, Foresman	_____	___	___	___	___
	_____	___	___	___	___
	_____	___	___	___	___
Harper Row	_____	___	___	___	___
	_____	___	___	___	___
	_____	___	___	___	___
Macmillan	_____	___	___	___	___
	_____	___	___	___	___
	_____	___	___	___	___
American Book	_____	___	___	___	___
	_____	___	___	___	___
	_____	___	___	___	___
Ginn	_____	___	___	___	___
	_____	___	___	___	___
	_____	___	___	___	___
Houghton-Mifflin	_____	___	___	___	___
	_____	___	___	___	___
	_____	___	___	___	___
Lippincott	_____	___	___	___	___
	_____	___	___	___	___
	_____	___	___	___	___

Series Titles (specify)	Use as major resource in teaching reading	Use as supplemental or optional course in class	Occasionally refer to myself but don't use in class	Don't use at all
Allyn & Bacon _____	___	___	___	___
_____	___	___	___	___
_____	___	___	___	___
Holt, Rinehart & Winston _____	___	___	___	___
_____	___	___	___	___
_____	___	___	___	___
SRA _____	___	___	___	___
_____	___	___	___	___
_____	___	___	___	___
Harcourt Brace Jovanovich _____	___	___	___	___
_____	___	___	___	___
_____	___	___	___	___
Open Court _____	___	___	___	___
_____	___	___	___	___
_____	___	___	___	___
ITA _____	___	___	___	___
_____	___	___	___	___
_____	___	___	___	___
Merrill Linguistics _____	___	___	___	___
_____	___	___	___	___
_____	___	___	___	___

41. Do you create any of the materials you use in teaching compensatory reading?

    1. ____ Yes

    2. ____ No

        a. If yes, which of the following types of materials do you create? (Check all that apply.)

           ____ Worksheets

           ____ Printed stories, poems, or essays

           ____ Transparencies for overhead projector

           ____ Filmstrips

           ____ Slides

           ____ Motion Pictures

           ____ Charts

           ____ Tapes

           ____ Other (specify) _____

42. How would you rate each of the following activities in terms of importance to you as goals in your current teaching of compensatory reading?

	Major Goal	Secondary Goal	Of Little or No Importance as a Goal
Improving motor abilities related to reading	____	____	____
Increasing attention span	____	____	____
Developing auditory discrimination	____	____	____
Matching letters or words	____	____	____
Learning letter forms	____	____	____
Developing a sight vocabulary (whole word recognition)	____	____	____
Learning word meanings (vocabulary)	____	____	____
Phonic and/or structural analysis	____	____	____

	Major Goal	Secondary Goal	Of Little or No Importance as a Goal
Developing skill in using context clues	___	___	___
Practicing syllabification skills	___	___	___
Practicing punctuation and paragraph skills	___	___	___
Developing comprehension skills	___	___	___
Developing comprehension skills	___	___	___
Improving comprehension rate	___	___	___
Developing listening skills	___	___	___
Reading aloud	___	___	___
Reading silently (independent silent reading)	___	___	___
Developing study skills	___	___	___
Developing library skills	___	___	___
Improving verbal communication	___	___	___
Creative writing	___	___	___
Reading for enjoyment	___	___	___
Enriching cultural background	___	___	___
Improving self-image	___	___	___
Improving attitudes toward reading	___	___	___
Other (specify) _____			
_____	___	___	___

43. About how often does each child in your compensatory reading class have the opportunity to read aloud to the class?

    ___ At least once a day

    ___ Several times a week, but not daily

_____ About once a week

_____ Less than once a week, but regularly

_____ Seldom or never on a regular basis

44. About how often does each child in your compensatory reading class have the opportunity to read aloud to you alone (or to another adult)?

     _____ At least once a day

     _____ Several times a week, but not daily

     _____ About once a week

     _____ Less than once a week, but regularly

     _____ Seldom or never on a regular basis

45. How successful would you consider your compensatory reading teaching to be with respect to each of the following criteria?

	Highly Successful	Moderately Successful	Moderately Unsuccessful	Totally Unsuccessful
Enhancing prereading skills	_____	_____	_____	_____
Enhancing measured reading achievement	_____	_____	_____	_____
Improving attitudes toward reading	_____	_____	_____	_____
Improving students' self-images	_____	_____	_____	_____
Remediating cultural deprivation	_____	_____	_____	_____